Kiss Me Again

A Memoir of Elgar in Unusual Places

by Alda Dizdari

To Eileen and Julian
With best wishes
Alda Dizdari

14/10/18

PublishNation
www.publishnation.co.uk

To Peter
for being there every step of the way

As a child, after hearing me complain about the violin and the frustrating hours I was spending practicing, my father took me by his side and said "Alda, do you see these four strings, on this small violin? Today they are short and they don't look like much, but one day they will be so long, and they will take you anywhere you want. They will make your life wonderful and magical. Keep playing them. They hold the secret to your life".

CONTENTS

CHAPTERS

TRACKS

Throughout the book there are references to excerpts from Elgar's Violin Concerto. These are links to the author's website where you can hear her performing the music.

https://aldadizdari.co.uk/elgartracks/

https://aldadizdari.co.uk/elgartracks/track-1/

https://aldadizdari.co.uk/elgartracks/track-2/

https://aldadizdari.co.uk/elgartracks/track-3/

https://aldadizdari.co.uk/elgartracks/track-4/

https://aldadizdari.co.uk/elgartracks/track-5/

https://aldadizdari.co.uk/elgartracks/track-6/

https://aldadizdari.co.uk/elgartracks/track-7/

https://aldadizdari.co.uk/elgartracks/track-8/

https://aldadizdari.co.uk/elgartracks/track-9/

https://aldadizdari.co.uk/elgartracks/track-10/

https://aldadizdari.co.uk/elgartracks/track-11/

https://aldadizdari.co.uk/elgartracks/track-12/

Preface

It all started in a vintage record shop near Oxford Street. While browsing I came across a recording of Elgar's Violin Concerto with Albert Sammons and Henry Wood conducting the New Queen's Hall Orchestra. I was going through an exploratory phase of listening to old recordings, trying to capture the sounds and gestures that are lost to the modern performer and I thought this would be an interesting start to discovering this work, performed more authentically by people who knew Elgar personally. On the same day, I found myself in Cecil Court, in another shop that sold old scores and as if in an act of faith, I found a copy of Elgar's Violin Concerto that once belonged to Henry Wood. The violin part was completely virgin but the piano part was heavily marked with his blue pencil. All the tempo indications and dynamics were circled and the timing for every movement clearly notated. I couldn't believe my eyes. There was a clear serendipity to all this. I bought the score although quite a dear purchase and the rest was already settled. What followed were two years of discovering the piece, of listening to recordings and looking for opportunities to perform this work. The journey was interesting. Most orchestras in Eastern Europe had played Elgar's Cello Concerto but didn't even know about the violin concerto. From very early on we received great support from the Elgar Society and my dream was to premiere it in Albania, my home country and in parts of Romania where I knew this work had either never or rarely been performed. It was indeed a journey worth taking. What I hadn't planned for though was the deeper meaning that evolved, more far-reaching than just the music. Not only was I discovering music I loved, I was also connecting with my past, and forging an even stronger link between my past, present and future.

It might have started as a great coincidence, in many ways, but my reaction to Elgar and his music, the way he has changed my music making and the way I see things now has been the biggest surprise of my life. While preparing for my performances I immersed myself in his life and the greatest impact came from Elgar himself, his writing and letters to his friends, especially his editor at Novello, August Jaeger, to whom he wrote on an almost daily basis and to whom he dedicated one of his most beautiful movements in the

Enigma Variations, "Nimrod". Another important source was his correspondence with friend and muse, Alice Stuart-Wortley, to whom he wrote many letters, especially the Windflowers Letters which gave me such an insight into Elgar's thinking. Elgar was speaking to me on many levels, by day through his musical ideas, which I had started to love with all my being, and by night through the letters, he sent to all his friends and supporters. Some of the most tender moments were revealed by his closest musician friend, W.H.Reed (or Billy as Elgar used to call him). Much of Elgar's personality was depicted so beautifully in Reed's memoir that, by the end of his first chapter, when reading the description of Elgar's death, I found myself in tears, as if he had been a close relative of mine who had just died all over again. It is funny how close you can get to a composer, to his soul. Elgar's eccentricities, the funny little stories about him turning all the paintings in his rented accommodation the wrong way round, or his odd experiments playing the chemist and blowing things up, or his long journeys into the woods and his incredible memory about every detail, of every place he had ever been, every person he had ever spoken to or encountered. All those details brought him even closer to my life as if I had a moving picture of his life accompanied by a beautiful soundtrack of his music. After reading Billy Reed's account of him, I even had an idea of the music that Elgar liked to listen to.*

The process of discovering Elgar's music and life has in itself been an exploration of myself and my life today. Bringing Elgar to 'unusual places' gave me an opportunity to discover or rediscover those places, gaining another meaning and understanding of my life. On a human level, the journey with Elgar represents much more than his music, it has been an opportunity of re-evaluating a world I thought I knew through new eyes as if shedding off my skin and stepping into another body, examining events and stories from a different perspective. I am still growing with this piece and may this journey never end. As performers in our musical journey, we often think of the composers we are studying as companions, almost closer to our core than the people in our day to day life. Elgar's humanity and his unique courage in discovering music his own way, on his own terms, has been my greatest inspiration to date. His music teaches me everything I need to know about beauty, humanity, passion and love.

"Kiss me again, a memoir of Elgar in unusual places" is a title I came up with after reading about his life and after being in places I didn't know but felt that I knew. This is in many ways a kiss with the past while moving into the future, it is a love story, with places I have left and revisited, of things I have loved and miss, and of music that is the continuous companion in this life's journey.

* In his book "Elgar as I knew him" by W.H.Reed, there is a detailed account of stories that he heard or was present as they unfolded. He also gives a comprehensive account of Elgar's musical tastes, composers he loved and was inspired by.

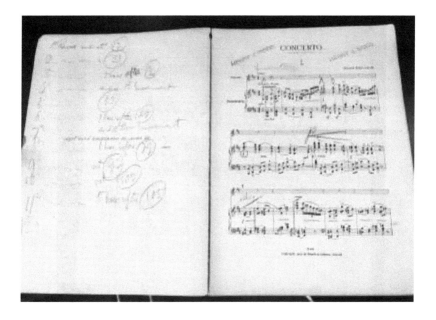

Henry Wood score of Elgar Violin Concerto ...

... and cover of the score.

Edward Elgar

Windflowers

Chapter 1

The journey began in not such an unusual place - Oxford, November 2015

The morning was dark and rainy. We left London and headed towards the North Circular and the M40 to Oxford. The shocking news was still sinking in and we didn't talk much in the car. Gloomy thoughts overwhelmed us. We were heading towards an exciting new experience but our hearts were heavy. My mind was filled with images from the Paris attack of the night before. It was very hard to digest. I could not get over the thought of all those innocent people heading out for a good night in the city or a meal with family and friends being slaughtered without mercy. The world had never felt gloomier. Paris, the city of love and romance, the city you always escape to when you need to capture that fine line of perfection, the city filled with people that know how to enjoy life. Paris, the city I always thought I had lived in in a previous life, had been under a terrorist attack.

As we approached Oxford my mind started to drift back to the task at hand. It had been two years since I had started working on Elgar's Violin Concerto and this was going to be the first in what I hoped would be a long journey with this piece. How many times had I contemplated that day, all the hours of practice and rehearsals with piano, the study of the score and the thinking about solutions to timings and tempo. It was finally time for me to actually play this piece in public with an orchestra.

Somehow Paris was overshadowing this important day with

thoughts that there was something larger than music, human life was more important. We arrived in Oxford around 11 o'clock but the darkness and the rain persisted. We parked the car and made our way to the hall.

Performing with an amateur orchestra, in a school, was never going to be a grand occasion, just a good preparation for what was to follow soon. The school had a lovely concert hall and good facilities. It was a small enough affair to give me an opportunity to run things through without feeling too pressured, and to see what needed to happen next and how it all came together.

The musicians started making their way to the hall. I opened my violin and began to warm up. I switched on to my other life, the musical life, my third arm made of wood firmly attached to my chin with every inch of my body prepared to honour this arm and give it the right access to the soul.

The mood was palpable, everybody was shaken, people were not talking much. They were all getting ready to start the rehearsal but their minds were elsewhere.

The conductor, Alexander Walker, a good friend of mine, came into the room and hurried to his platform, his forehead beaded with perspiration. In his jolly voice, where you could hardly distinguish the humour from sadness, as though personal emotions were somehow shameful, he said: 'Can you believe it?'. There was no reply to his question, just a sigh.

The Leader took her seat. She was a lovely lady and probably the only professional musician in the section. She stood up and the orchestra went silent, the oboe played an A and they all tuned. I was still in awe of this Britishness, the way people in this country take on events, inwardly, as if perplexed but unable to express verbally their inner feelings. If I was standing in front of an orchestra anywhere else in Europe, probably with only one exception, Germany, we would have spent at least 15 minutes talking about the news, the events, the images, the horror, fear, anger. A state of collective mourning would have made the day very exciting but useless. Instead, I was standing in front of a calm group of people who had sacrificed their precious Saturday to rehearse and perform the Elgar Violin Concerto.

When the music started, within the first few bars it took us into a different place. There was not a single unnecessary note. The orchestral introduction weaves all the main themes of the piece, engaging all the instruments in a dialogue that guarantees an hour of the most profound human interaction. Before the solo violin has played a single note you feel you have already climbed a mountain.
(Track 1 - First Movement - Orchestral Introduction)
https://aldadizdari.co.uk/elgartracks/track-1/

I had spent many months thinking about those first few bars of the solo entrance after the orchestral introduction, what they mean, how to approach them. The best help came from Elgar himself. There is no point in trying to glean information from outside the source, like reading somebody's description of Marmite. The only source of the truth, especially with works written well by composers who know how to write and what they want, is the taste, the score.
Elgar is very precise about this beginning. After the lengthy introduction the solo violin comes in like a human voice and the first theme, the first Windflower theme, named as such by Elgar himself, appears, but not in its original form and not complete, just the last fragment, like the conclusion of an idea and not the statement. It is the start of many novelties Elgar introduced in this work, that contributed to creating a myth but made it also misunderstood by many. The first theme is placed

in a warm, beautiful and rich register of the violin on G string that gives the violinist a great opportunity for expressiveness. The theme is like a recitativo, the violin searching and exploring and the music sometimes meditative and inward looking. But very soon it is moving forward and rising up, contracting and expanding with great agility, while the orchestra lingers in the background. The first theme develops with great panache and virtuosic passages between the orchestra and the soloist, starting a much bigger conversation. (Track 2 - First Movement - First Windflower Theme)
https://aldadizdari.co.uk/elgartracks/track-2/

After years of performing and teaching I had finally realised the interpreter's real duty and challenge. The real challenge is translating the score and giving Elgar's clear notation and directions a musical sense. The truth emerges from the data getting absorbed to such a degree that you create the music completely guided by these notations to the point you take the shape of the music, you ARE music, the phrases flow from you yet they are not you, as if your spirit has been captured by another spirit and you are the vehicle. This is the way we can be transported in time. It takes an enormous effort by all parties involved, the composer writing the score, the performer learning the score, the audience reacting to the score.

On this occasion, the orchestra sometimes played out of tune and many virtuosic passages were difficult for them but we were all in a state of ecstasy with this music. How can it be possible to love every note in a piece? Almost an hour of absolute bliss. Everything was a little raw and I noticed so many things that were not working yet in my playing and in relation to the orchestra, but the beauty of the melodies, the structure, and above all, the incredible colours in the music made this piece breathtakingly beautiful. I counted my blessings. When we finished we were all smiling. A different energy surrounded us, we felt warmth and love towards each other, a brotherhood of men. For one hour we hadn't thought about Paris or the horrendous things people can do to other people. For one hour we had been in Edwardian England, surrounded by noble feelings and beautiful scenery. Elgar had lovingly taken us on a walk around the places he loved, the Malvern Hills in the springtime, guiding us through fields filled with windflowers, and with a childlike energy and wonder, shown us a glimpse of eternal youth. A vision of delight and hope. Suddenly this was not a sacrificed Saturday but an essential survival tool, life made sense in music and we all had a meaning.

We left the building where the rehearsal took place. Outside it was still dark and a thick cloud was hanging over the city but it was not raining. We went in search of a local pub for a light lunch. Thanks to the wonders of the internet we found a small independent pub that offered very good food, including pork crackling and scotch eggs, though I decided on a traditional fish and chips menu. You don't want to be too adventurous with food before a performance.

I was feeling much better after the rehearsal and started to feel the adrenaline rising in preparation for the concert. Everything about a performance, it doesn't matter how big or small, gives a new dimension to existence. As a performer you feel as if you live your life through these frames, practicing for a concert, rehearsing with a piano or ensemble for the concert, selecting a dress for the performance, packing the music and clothes for the concert, making your way to the venue, all the logistical details relating to any performance. Until the moment of walking on stage you remember every little element and in the mind, a canvas has been created, a perfectly formed event that from the micro to the macro level will be forever remembered and which time will not erase.

The lunch in the pub had been delicious, a great reminder of the lovely place Oxford really is. I had visited Oxford for the first time in 2005, while leading the Allegri String Quartet, one of the oldest string quartets in the country. I loved this city of culture. In some parallel universe, I felt I had lived and studied here. The old colleges had been my stomping ground. I fancied myself a member of its intelligent population, walking purposefully amongst all those clever people with their heads full of high pursuits and their awkwardness caused by their privileged upbringing. Somehow I felt I had to be a student of English literature, how could it be otherwise? In my mind, I had written many books and this had been my starting point. My encounter with the works of Evelyn Waugh only confirmed this conviction. I loved every minute of Brideshead Revisited, especially the BBC series. For me, it had been an incredible insight into the world of the English aristocracy, their eccentricities. With the main character Charles Ryder I shared such a strong sense of being an outsider in this world. I was destined to be an outsider wherever I went, even back home in Albania, and I liked to find kindred souls, people who bore the same signs, longing and expression.

I think I loved Elgar even more because of his inability to fit in. I could see him as another outsider, somebody who felt all his life he wasn't good enough, not aristocratic enough, didn't belong to the great German tradition, didn't like to be at the centre of the London world. He didn't study with the great composers of the time, instead, he studied the masters by copying their scores or creating music using their techniques and relied completely on his originality and musical instinct. I also felt we were kindred souls for the simplest reason that we both were born one day apart in June, both Gemini with the twins firmly imprinted in our character.

The day had started tragically but developed in the most remarkable way, with a good rehearsal, a lovely meal and by the time we left the pub and headed for the concert hall, even the weather had improved and turned into a lovely afternoon and early evening. The trees reflected wonderful autumn colours on the water. I felt really inspired. The atmosphere reminded me so much of the works of one of my favourite British artists, Richard Robbins, who I was really lucky to meet in the last years of his life. Richard was an incredibly sensitive artist, deeply inspired by music and nature. He constantly painted to music and sometimes the music had such a strong influence on his art it became one of the main pillars of inspiration in his work. His paintings were often abstract yet specific, and they touched you the way music does, in a very personal way, they had movement and were evocative. Looking at the colours and movements of the water, with all my nostalgic thoughts about Oxford, which had once been Richard's world, made me miss him so much I could almost feel his presence in the place.

At around 6.30 pm I went into the green room to warm up and change into my new vintage dress, a gift from my very dear friends and next door neighbours. I was surrounded by friends who bought me dresses. From the moment they realised I loved vintage dresses and preferred to perform in them, they kept supplying me with dresses from all over the country. This one had come from a shop in Brighton. I am convinced that vintage shops offer the best shopping experience all over the world. I talked so much about this that not long afterwards my friends started to visit them too and we would have little competitions for the best bargains. We were constantly trying to outdo each other. Usually, I was the winner, as most of the time, I got to wear the dresses. But what a coincidence that the latest vintage purchase was a dress filled with windflowers made out of black lace woven on cream colour silk. As soon as I saw it I knew what I was going to wear for my first Elgar concert in Oxford. After all, Elgar had named two of the concerto's main themes, The Windflower Themes.

An even stranger experience had happened to me during a trip down to the South East of England in Kent a few weeks prior to the concert in Oxford. Walking through a small antique market in the heart of a little town called Faversham, I spotted a rather special dress hanging in the rails. The dress was made of velvet and had an incredible shape, very much inspired by a Tudor dress, a style heavily imitated by the Edwardians, with a beautiful décolleté crusted with tiny red stones all around and a long train at the back. The colour was an unusual shiny grey/aubergine. I examined the dress closely. It was an original costume from the performance of Richard Strauss' Salome at the English National Opera. It had been tailored for the lead role. I couldn't believe my eyes, this piece was created for a production of a work written only a few years before the concerto, with the libretto based on the work by Oscar Wilde. Furthermore, Elgar, when asked by some conservative Americans to join a complaint against Salome being performed in New York in the 20s, had declared Richard Strauss a genius of the times.

I bought the dress on the spot, it cost me just £10. Not only had I a piece of English history in my hands but I had also found the perfect outfit for the premiere of the concerto in Albania.

Sometimes I wonder if there is such a thing as chance, luck? Sometimes I just think everything is predestined and we follow a path that is already laid out for us. More and more I have proof of a greater force, a calling of our desires, and all my dreams follow a road to reality. Most of the time that road is long and hard, and by the time I get there I feel I have forgotten the dream, but these days I know I shouldn't. It is very heartwarming to remind ourselves that dreams can come true, eventually.

The orchestra was already in place and the leader had tuned it. The big moment had arrived. The audience fell silent as we made our way on stage. Elgar, here we go.

The performance was far from perfect. There were still a lot of passages for me to work on and clean up, and many places where the orchestra and conductor could improve, but the overall feeling was right. I was trying to play exactly what was written on the page, and while doing so I was wondering how much I should temper the markings, how I should organise the accelerandos or ritenutos, how I could get the right balance. The answer is not simple. To translate a score correctly it is not enough just to translate the markings, one also has to give them an emotional sense without making them artificial. After all, music is not an action but a spiritual state.

Richard Robbins once told me a quote by the philosopher Walter Pater that I loved: "Art constantly aspires to the condition of music. Art is always trying to unify form and subject, in music form and subject are seamlessly one."

This quote sums up what I feel about music and here, in the Elgar Violin Concerto, was a work where subject and form lived and breathed in great harmony and brought a spirituality that was very much in line with Wagner operas or Brahms symphonies.

The audience loved the work despite the length. Everybody was so enthusiastic about this little-performed gem. In the audience, I spotted one of my young students, one of those extremely intelligent individuals who make you feel much more optimistic about the world and its future. Her clever face was full of hidden passion and she made up for her small stature with a great and vibrant spirit. She seemed deeply moved and inspired by the piece. It was also special to have in the audience one of my great supporters. His words afterwards were very encouraging and they made me feel more optimistic about the path I was on. I knew they came from a place of deep understanding and knowledge.

I had two weeks to prepare for Albania, and driving back to London I kept singing the Windflower themes. Life seemed wonderful.

The little sunken garden in Tirana with the Skanderbeg statue during communist times. The Boulevard is to the left.

A proud survivor, Skanderbeg today.

Tirana overlooked by Mount Dajti in the background.

May Day parade 1987: the author with Nexhmije Hoxha,
the wife of the deceased dictator - a proud moment!

The author with her father at his piano ...

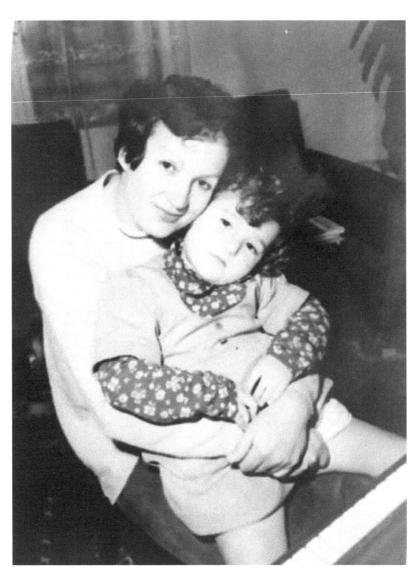

... and with her mother.

Chapter 2

Elgar in Tirana - A kiss with the past
November 2015

Elgar is not a well-known composer in Eastern Europe. When I was growing up in the late 80s for most Eastern Europeans Great Britain was a faraway island covered in fog and rain where children suffered like in Dickens' stories. During communism, those were the great impressions we had of England and we knew almost nothing about Wales, Ireland and Scotland apart from the kilts most Scotsmen wore which made them really strange people. It is no surprise that Elgar's Violin Concerto had never reached Albania. This was a great opportunity for me, a genuine lover of the music of Elgar. After much negotiation with the directors in the national radio and television orchestra of the Albanian state and with much help from the Albanian Ambassador in London, Mr Mal Berisha, we finally had a date and an orchestra. We even received support from the Elgar Society of Great Britain dedicated to promoting the works of the great composer.

However, not even the slightest interest was shown by the British Council or the British Embassy in Albania. Despite regular emails and efforts to draw their attention, we failed to capture their imagination.

The concert was scheduled to take place on the 28th of November, on the Albanian National Day.

For me, this was of great significance. It was a good opportunity to celebrate this work in the same style we celebrate our national day. After all, the two events took place only two years apart, the concerto was written in 1910 and

Albania won its independence from the Ottoman Empire in 1912. I couldn't help draw a parallel between the two worlds that were facing me, on one hand, a civilised, rich, sophisticated world, and on the other hand a country with a long and bloodied struggle for survival bearing the pains and hardships that most small countries have to endure, overshadowed and controlled by powerful nations.

How would it be to collide these worlds? How would Albania receive the world of Elgar? I was so excited. In my naive and romantic view of the world, I thought this would be a great occasion for celebration by all parties.

Preparations were going well, the concerto was coming along nicely and gaining gravitas so I was not concerned when my mother showed some scepticism regarding the choice of the date.

We travelled to Tirana well in advance to ensure we had plenty of time to prepare the orchestra for the performance. I was happy to go back to my childhood place, to see my city and meet my family and friends. Everything had changed in Tirana, old connections were gone but deep inside I felt these streets were still mine. I didn't belong there anymore but the streets recognised me.

What is home? Is it a city? Is it the language you speak, the food you eat, the people you love or the space you sleep in?

...

Where was home? I had left Tirana at the age of 15, I had lived longer abroad and I was almost scared of my abilities to speak the language correctly, after all, during these years, language, like people, had evolved in ways I couldn't possibly foresee.

I don't know if Tirana is a beautiful city or not as I still see it with my old eyes. The ancient buildings, the communist housing blocks, Lana, the little river that runs through the centre of the city that is a miniature of a river and has its own charms, the bridges that connect Lana. Everything is linked to a story. My favourite bridge used to be a little pedestrian crossing that connected two main streets. I used to stop there in the middle of the bridge and eat ice cream with my best friend. We would contemplate life and imagine so many alternative futures for ourselves. She left Albania almost as early as I did but I have such strong recollections of our chats that Tirana of my teenage years is directly linked to her.

Tirana, during the transitional years, transformed and changed more than most ex-communist countries I know. Every year I returned from my studies abroad to find a city completely transformed. One year I came home to find both banks of the Lana completely occupied by illegal buildings. Every little space, every green space in the centre of the city had been taken over by kiosks that sold food, roasted chickens, pizzas. Everybody was eating constantly. It was the year I saw the biggest change in people, my friends being transformed from thin youngsters into fat people with big tummies and thick necks. In the space of one year, they had changed so much they were sometimes unrecognisable.

Tirana resembled the vision I had of Paris in the Middle Ages, dirty and chaotic, with no urban planning, the people too preoccupied with forgetting about their past and wiping everything that represented the old regime. We were entering a new age, and I felt more of an outsider than ever. My childhood city was gone, and with it, my romantic perception of my homeland. In 1997 Albania entered a deep and traumatising period of social unrest. After the collapse of a series of disastrous pyramid schemes, Tirana was a city in distress. You could buy Kalashnikovs in any city in Albania and I even saw, on one of the main streets of Tirana, a tank for sale. Every wedding was celebrated by firing guns and many people were accidentally killed or injured by blind bullets. During those dark times, children were the most affected. With long energy cuts, limited water supply, the sound of guns and the dark and violent energy around, what could this city offer to its children? It was in those days that my pianist mother started a music competition, mainly to offer a purpose, distraction and platform for the children of Tirana. Music, once again, as throughout my life growing up in Albania, had become the healing vehicle. Music had again resurrected dreams and brought beauty into young lives, and hope for a better future.

Some cities have very short memory but the only thing that hasn't changed in Tirana is the big boulevard. These days Tirana gives out vibes of order and calm. A new Mayor with some artistic vision had painted old, tired and sad buildings in strange colours and patterns, almost a caricature or a joke on the brutalist communist architecture. Then he demolished all the illegal buildings on the banks of the Lana and in the national park. He planted new trees and flowers in the parks but the damage had been done. All the old trees, the weeping willows and mimosa trees that so beautifully surrounded the little streets were gone forever. They represented the past nobody wanted to remember. One area in that boulevard had been the subject of much debating. During the communism period, at the centre of the boulevard, near the Old Mosque and the History Museum there used to be a little sunken garden with lots of green surrounding the platform of the garden, and at the top of the garden, there was a beautiful and proud sculpture of our national hero, Skanderbeg. He saw it all, the May Parades, the crowds that demolished the statue of our dictator, Enver Hoxha, the crowds that elected the first democratic party, the crowds that destroyed Tirana and soon he himself was threatened with change as the planners in the Mayor's office decided the fate of the new Tirana. Many debated and a lot of plans were drawn up about this transformation. After much work and lots of public funding spent, the garden was given a "due makeover". The place we all recalled in our family albums as being, during communism, the only place you could have a picture taken outdoors, was going to vanish forever. Every Albanian, whether from Tirana or not, had a picture of themselves taken in that garden, usually tightly squeezing a relative or sibling, badly dressed but with beaming smiles and with Skanderbeg in the background. They were wiping that memory too and we even feared for the fate of Skanderbeg himself, hoping that such a national figure would be spared. The new makeover was a flat and horrible non-structure that locals started calling "Lines", a local brand of a sanitary napkin, as it resembled one as seen from the air. Another mayor soon after scrapped the newly made over square and resurrected the old plans drawn up by the Italians in the 30s. Yet again poor Skanderbeg was covered by scaffolding and returned to a younger version of the old sunken garden with brand new trees that looked so new you could have mistaken the place for some emerging Arab Super Casino Resort.

...

Now here I was again arriving at the latest Tirana, with my mission to introduce Elgar to my compatriots.

As we started our descent into the Mother Teresa Airport I observed the houses, some still not fully completed. They had been abandoned or left incomplete for as long as I had travelled back and forth. They gave an air of unfinished business to the whole area. Tirana is surrounded by hills and mountains, the biggest just above it being Mount Dajti. The land around the airport is divided into strips and looks very uneven, but the hills and mountains are beautiful. As soon as I saw them I felt my heart racing. It meant I was going to see my parents very soon.

...

I had realised from very early on in my life that whenever I lived in Tirana, even as a child, all I ever wanted was to be left alone, not to draw attention, not to be a target but to just be free to exist in my own mind without having to deal with the expectations of others. Maybe that was because I had a famous father and our world revolved around him and his dreams, or maybe because many people envied us and we were the targets of a lot of jealousy.

And maybe it was because we were constantly surrounded by people who were watching us. At work and school, everybody was monitored. You had to conform, even your haircut had to be common and undistinguished. At home, the Fronti Nacionial, an Albanian resistance organization that fought in World War II, mainly run now by pensioners, was even more enthusiastic about controlling your moves. So much so that on the only free day of the week, a Sunday morning, everybody had to go out and clean the areas around the building blocks where we lived. It was an excellent way for those bored and vicious old people to keep a secure grip on any foreign behaviour. I remember some very funny moments from those times. Now that I think about them they send shivers down my spine but back then, as a kid of around five or six, I found them quite amusing.

We lived in a building constructed by the Italian government for Italian officials working in Albania after the invasion in the 30s. They were elegant apartments with high ceilings and marble entrances, equipped with central heating, and every apartment had one room in the basement for storing the coal. The three-floor apartment buildings had lovely terraces overlooking the street on one side, tennis courts on the other and gardens front and back with magnolia and palm trees. I loved those buildings. They had so many places to hide and so much open space to run around. Since the buildings were in the centre of the city but felt quite secluded and protected, often couples would come and hide discretely and enjoy some intimacy away from prying eyes. But nobody could escape the eagle eyes of the national front. Often the whole block would be shaken by screams. We would all jump and go out to see poor couples being shoved out of hiding places with brooms, followed by a lot of verbal abuse. The leader of the movement was a guy called Vasili and on the days when he was not throwing boiling lead from the terrace to the basement to make bullets for his hunting hobby, he was busy policing the movements of lovers. I can never forget his pervert's thick glasses. While hitting them with brooms he had a very proud and contented face. I am sure he loved to see them in action, it was probably his version of live pornography.

On election days we were awoken to an atmosphere of great euphoria. The sooner you went to vote the more devoted you were seen to be to the great cause. As a result, nobody slept. The entire building was in pandemonium and for us children, it was a great opportunity to stay up all night and play outside. The voting took place in the basement of one of the buildings. The results were always the same, the party had won by 99% of the votes. I am sure many wondered why we even bothered to vote.

There was another way of enjoying life though, one I

discovered very early on, a parallel world where I wasn't disturbed by others, even loved ones. In that world, I was free to wonder, to discover the world with my own eyes, to be curious and above all, to dream. That world was found in books and music.

Somehow reading or playing music was the only way to disconnect from that close knitted web that people had constructed in their lives and those of others. That didn't exist when I read or played the violin and sometime I would choose to do both at the same time. I would take some action story or murder mystery book, put it on my music stand and read while pretending to play so I didn't arouse suspicion in my mother. I would stay around four-five hours in the furthest room in the house, spending time in complete bliss. It got even better when I discovered a drink that we called Orange Punch, made out of orange juice and a lot of sugar and alcohol. At the age of around 11, I had no idea that the drink was alcoholic. I had seen my mother being served that liquor when we went to visit her friends and I was always annoyed that they never offered me any. So, when I discovered we had some in the house I made it my daily routine to take some into my hiding den to enjoy with the rest of my favourite activities, until one day my oldest sister discovered me and, to her shock, had the first glimpse of my rebellious side.

…

Now I was back in Tirana, an adult, arriving at the new apartment where my parents live these days. It is not the big and glorious apartment of my childhood, but a sad little modern apartment in a good part of town called "Bllok" where, during communism, the members of the party used to live. The beautiful Italian apartment blocks have been transformed like the rest of this city. The first shock wave of change came when

I was 14 and had gone abroad for the first time performing with my school's string ensemble. We went to Corfu and met lots of other children who admired our musical talent. The week in Corfu was one of the happiest in my memory. I shall never forget the day I arrived back home though. Tirana was very poor in those days and part of that was obvious in the lack of lighting on the streets. Evenings could seem terribly dark in Tirana. When I entered my building I felt quite scared of the darkness and I called for my mother. After calling for her many times I made my way through the dark staircase to the third floor where we lived in number 36 and saw the door of our apartment wide open. At the end of the corridor, I saw the piano where my father had composed all his life. A strange looking lady was washing the floors of the apartment, but I didn't know her. For a very brief moment, I thought I was in a dream or I had got the address wrong. And with a trembling voice, I just asked her: 'Is this the house of the Dizdari Family?' to which she responded in a loud and irritated voice 'Yes, this is it, but they are nowhere to be seen!'. And that is how I found out that our apartment had been forcefully occupied by other people. My parents, in protest, had left all our belongings and hadn't returned home for the entire week I had been having such a lovely time in Greece. That was the first glimpse of the times that were coming. Our family had been targeted as an elite that needed crushing. In the political landscape of the time, my father had positioned himself in the opposition party, a member of the Socialist Party. We had been bullied for months and asked to vacate some of the rooms in our flat to people arriving from labour camps or political dissidents arriving from some far away places. My father was determined to fight for his legal rights through the courts of justice and, in the end, he won, but for me, it was too late. I lost my old Tirana forever and after that my life in that city was not safe anymore and I had to leave and study abroad.

25

...

My heart aches when I see how my parents get older every time I see them, they become so precious. Now I see them as children that need caring for while they see me as their child they need to care for. It is a tricky dynamic. In the effort to establish some control over the situation my mother had cooked and prepared a feast as if she was expecting her hungry teenager to arrive from the war. I politely tried everything she had prepared and was amazed at her ability to bring back the child in me with one lift of the spoon. Parents, they are special all over the world, but the family relations in a country like Albania are on a completely different level. They reflect the isolation, poverty, longing, pain and all the sacrifices everyone had to make to be able to survive.

I went to bed with my head empty of Elgar, I was overwhelmed by Albania, it was an avalanche of feelings that almost choked me every time. As if the carefully pressurised bottle was opened and what once used to be my reality, this tiny universe called Albania, this world you can only understand if you have lived in it, returned and sucked me in. I went to sleep with the smell of the conditioner my mother had washed the sheets with, it was the closest thing to a teddy bear.

...

The first thing I saw when I woke up in the morning was mount Dajti. Again I asked myself, is it a beautiful mountain or is it because I love it? The mount looked like a mantelpiece around Tirana, you could enjoy the sky and the clouds as they moved and played with the mountain and the colours changed all the time.

My parents had been awake since 6am, they had already

completed the ritual of coffee drinking and my father had finished his morning routine which was quite noisy. He has lived without caring for others for far too long to mind his footsteps. In many ways, he is still the king of the castle and we all have to accept that.

I could feel their excitement, complete happiness. My mother was already nervous about my day. She kept calling me; 'My brave little daughter', as if what I was going to do was close to fighting on a battlefield or saving lives. It just showed the way they perceived music making. It was a battle for recognition, acceptance, survival and honour. Only now I could understand all my anxieties about performing and following my dream of being a concert violinist. If you start your life guided by fears, soon they take over your life.

I was trying to concentrate on the rehearsal. I had prepared as hard as I could to be able to face an orchestra, probably one of the toughest ones, because it was full of people that lived and thought like my mother.

The sun was shining. The air was crispy and fresh. November can be a beautiful month in Tirana. I walked out into the street and, disregarding my father's advice to take a taxi, instead walked, deeply inhaling the air, waking up the nostalgia. And Elgar was back in my nostrils. He became present. Elgar and nostalgia. What a combination. The Windflower themes are the most nostalgic phrases of music I have ever had the luck to play, and I say luck, absolute, complete, sublime luck that makes you pinch yourself. The second Windflower theme is so beautifully written and notated that I feel absolutely no fear about performing it because all my mental capacities are overtaken by the beauty and my mission to do it justice. This theme comes out of nowhere, like a sudden blooming of a little innocent flower on the spring grass. In the score, it is marked *Semplice and Pianissimo,* and it has to be the most simple tune as if sung by a child walking towards the flower. And then it is repeated again, this time still *P* but marked *expressivo,* as if you are coming closer to this flower and realising summer is approaching. The third time, however, the melody soars high and takes wing together with the orchestra and you are overwhelmed with the nostalgia of that first spring day, one particular morning walk, one particular sunrise and skyline. You can never forget or repeat that but you can repeat the feelings it left on you. I couldn't wait to play this piece, to hear the orchestra marvel at the same theme, or would they?

(Track 3 - First Movement - Second Windflower Theme)
https://aldadizdari.co.uk/elgartracks/track-3/

I crossed the big Boulevard, the same place I went to cross every day many years ago to go to school, the Music High School in Tirana. The route to the National Radio was exactly the same one as to the school, the Radio Building where the rehearsals took place was in front of the high school. This famous boulevard is connected to millions of lives that called it home. It saw many May the first parades full of excitement and celebrations for a doctrine people didn't dare to question. On this boulevard, I marched very proudly when only 5 years old and ran to present flowers to Nexhmije Hoxha, the wife of our communist leader/dictator. Recently my mother sent me a picture taken with her that day. My face radiates with happiness. I remember the evening before that day, I couldn't sleep. I had checked and rechecked a hundred times my special white socks, the uniform and red 'pioneer' scarf, all neatly arranged by my mother. She had taken some special time to arrange my unruly curly hair. It was still a mess in the morning and of course in the picture, I looked like a typical communist kid. But I remember the joy and the pride of being part of something so special.

While I have travelled half the globe and made my way through several schools and languages, most of my colleagues from that high school have moved only a few hundred meters and now work in the National Radio-Television Symphony Orchestra. I saw them all making their way into the building. I met them with warmth and joy but I also realised there was always a part of me I never shared with them or anybody else in those days. The part of me that today stands strong and happy was then hidden very deep. The free spirit, my biggest dream in life, was kept well hidden and guarded. All they saw was a not very loud outsider who tried to fit in but didn't quite manage it.

I had shared some very important moments with this orchestra, including one of the biggest events in my life, my performance in Canterbury Cathedral in 2008, as a soloist in the Canterbury Festival. They were in my life forever, as the group that had helped mark a milestone for me and I was in their lives forever as their countrywoman who brought them to Britain.

I greeted the conductor, the same positive and enthusiastic British musician who played with me in Oxford, and I felt so comfortable and hopeful that I had both worlds in the palm of my hand. And now we were going to play Elgar.

The orchestra took a while to calm down. It was the complete opposite of what happened in Oxford. Everybody had too much to talk about and this was their daily job, something they had to do, for which they didn't get paid much, really. In the orchestra, I saw quite a few new faces which I think is always a good thing, new energy, hopefully, new or renewed vision and aspirations. Finally, after at least 10 minutes of struggling to establish some order we were ready to start. They were reading this music for the very first time. I could see they were curious to find out more.

They could certainly play better than the amateur orchestra back in Oxford. Strings were strong, and they played with vigour the energetic passages at the beginning. The brass section, however, struggled a little with the tuning and holding the chords, but they too were happy to get their teeth into some new challenging repertoire. The woodwinds, with their old and very dated instruments, were managing alright reading but somehow the entire sound was excited and rather loud all the time, not allowing the music to really settle and be contemplative. We ran through all the movements helping the orchestra understand their parts and making sense of the music without throwing them in at the deep end. I finished playing and my entire body was aching. I had been forcing, trying to match the power of this big group. It can take a big toll on your muscles. Forcing the instrument and the music is like fighting gravity. You can never win. Only by understanding the laws of nature can we embrace humanity and deliver to our best ability.

The conductor was pleased with the first reading. He saw potential. We went out of the building and made our way to a local restaurant that was right across the road from my former high school.

...

How many days of laughter and careless attitude were spent inside those walls, and how many days of fear and darkness experienced at the gates of that high school. I was left with two very big impressions from those years. One was the joy I felt when spending time with my friends, playing in ensembles with them and laughing about almost anything, experiencing all those little butterflies when encountering along the hallways of the school our romantic little crushes. The other was the terror that lay outside. When leaving the school we were surrounded

30

by gangsters who watched us like hawks, finding any excuse to come and grab us by the arm or elbow and telling us how they had "A Fixation" on us. One moment of eye contact was enough to make them fancy you and then you had to be "their" girl and they would come and claim you as their fully entitled trophy. Even today I tend to walk with my head down, avoiding eye contact. I escaped unharmed back then but other friends were not so lucky. Some girls got raped, others spent almost every day at school hiding in the Headmaster's office as he was just as powerless in the face of armed criminals.

And still, looking at the school building from across the street, I realised the good had overcome the bad. I still had a smile on my face thinking of all the laughter that only youth can crown you with.

We had a delicious meal of Albanian dishes and my English colleague was delighted with this city but a bit puzzled by the attitude of the director of the orchestra who had shown every sign of being tricky and unreliable. He was baffled by the British establishment in Tirana which had shown no interest in this premiere of the work of the greatest British composer.

I assured him that all would be well in the end and made my way back home looking forward to seeing my parents.

They were waiting for me, excited and a little worried about the rehearsal. The news had already been broken to my father that my playing was in good shape and the orchestra was delighted to have us back. I took everything with a pinch of scepticism and smiled. My mother continued saying: 'My brave little daughter, my brave little daughter' while holding my hand in her agile and warm hand. I hugged her and could feel her body shrinking in my arms. She was definitely smaller these days. I went to put my father to bed, his daily siesta which he followed with religious devotion. They were again

31

little children and both sides were equally childlike towards each other. I didn't think I could introduce any adult conversation or behaviour, not yet, there was still too much hugging to be done.

I was a little worried about my hands and body. Everything was feeling sore. I had to find a way to settle into my playing and get in my zone. I spent all afternoon practising passages that didn't work in the rehearsal, knowing very well that the real reason was not the passages but the attitude. Somehow, like the rest of the orchestra, I was paddling through the concerto thinking about how difficult it was rather than pacing the music so that passages fell naturally into place. I was just realising how young I was with this piece. It was a new friend that I knew I loved but I didn't know why and how.

The next morning I was determined to make the necessary changes and improve my performance by not allowing the orchestra to push me around or by their sheer force to bully me into self-defence. The act of performing is so boundless, it encompasses everything you have been through, everything that has marked you. You can build a wall around you and fight your corner. You can feel the audience is your enemy, ready to judge you, kill you, mock you, and the only way to survive is by building a wall and from there fight to the dying hour. Performing is a scary activity that feels much more like a battlefield than a place of great energetic exchange. Most of the skills we build in the hours of practice are based around building muscle memory, of teaching the body how to take the punches and be invincible, so much of the work is about conquering the fear of performing. And yet, the truly great performances, or at least those that had left the biggest impact on me, had been those where there were no walls, there was no battlefield, where I experienced the strength and the vulnerability of performers, where I accompanied them through the tough moments as well as the glorious ones and together we had climbed all the way to the highest and the greatest energetic exchanges ever to exist. I had felt no fear when I experienced those performances, not even of death. I had felt the love, the absolute love. In those moments I felt I had a religion, and that religion, for a humanist like myself, was music. But orchestras can be cruel places. Most of the musicians have the killer instinct. It takes a lot of strength not to try and protect yourself, but to let them feel your love and weaknesses. The orchestras in Eastern Europe have had tough lives, even tougher stories than mine and they are not forgiving. Very often, even their sound takes the shape of their stories. This one was sharp and hard. It was the sound of a country that had not much time to enjoy itself, but most of the time had battled to survive.

As I neared the recording hall where the orchestra rehearsed I was suddenly struck by other sounds, equally powerful to me, the sounds of my father's symphony. His first symphony was the opening work in the programme we were preparing. I had grown up listening to his music, delivered on the piano by this passionate and slightly mad person. He was my hero, the larger than life character that our whole universe revolved around. He was charismatic and loud, and when he played the piano he sang at the same time and passion came out of him in waves that moved the entire house and of course carried our souls into a state of exultation and wonder. His symphony had been one of the first works as a child I had seen performed by an orchestra and it had left a big impact on me. There was always a side of my father that was very vulnerable and his melodies encapsulated so much longing that many of his colleagues called him the "Schubert of Albania". The themes stayed with you long after you heard them, and he did write a lot of songs and themes for very popular movies. He was, in his days of youthful glory, one of the most successful composers in Albania. Back then I saw him as a guiding light in this little universe we called Albania, and I could have never guessed the journey this young boy had made to get there. He often talked about poverty, the kind you only read about in books. There was always a mystery around his past and we never talked about his father, my grandfather. He didn't exist. As a child I was extremely fond of his mother, I used to spend hours, days in her bed with her, listening to her stories and taking in her scent. One day she took me to a playground and while she was putting me on a merry go round horse she had an accident and broke her leg; she never recovered from that. She died, leaving me with the guilty feeling that I had killed her, she died because of me. There was a strong bond between my father and me. I could feel his pain, his vulnerability and from very early on we shared a very special friend. Sibelius' Violin Concerto was our special bond. At the age of 5, I fell in love with this piece so badly I couldn't listen to it afterwards. For the longest time, I felt if I played it something tremendous would happen, like a death or something dreadful. There was something so dark, so deep as if a hidden corner of my soul had been exposed for all to see and the reaction was almost violent. My father's music had some of that melancholy and darkness. When I finally got up my courage to play Sibelius Violin Concerto it was for a very special occasion. It followed important moments in my life. I had moved into a country I loved, England, I had lost somebody that I loved very dearly, a childhood love and memory of my past. Sibelius was that little island of pain and hope that had brought music and the violin into my life and I could only celebrate this work in a cathedral like Canterbury accompanied by an Albanian Orchestra making their debut in the UK. In addition, they were starting the concert with my father's symphony. It was a big deal for all of us.

Approaching the doors of the rehearsal space in Tirana I was transported back to that day in Canterbury. While making my way slowly through the dark passages of the Cathedral, up some steep steps, passing the very place where Thomas a Becket had been assassinated, I could hear this Albanian folk tune, used as the main theme in the slow movement of my father's symphony. Like a precious thread, it was taking me back to my beloved childhood, to my first memory of my father, to the love of the sun and those fresh days in my city of Tirana. That simple melody was moving elegantly between the instruments, like a message of love and peace in a country that hasn't seen much of either. I definitely had to have a wall then, because I could have easily crumbled into a puddle of tears then and there. Instead, I made my way and played the concerto that had tormented me for so long and had started my journey with the violin, and which had created that special bond with my father.

Studying and reading about Elgar, I came to see so many similarities between him and my father. I found some of his vulnerability even more relatable. Like Elgar, my father was an outsider. He was an orphan with very dubious family circumstances. His father had been shot by the communists during the war. His mother came from a wealthy landowner's family. Her uncle had been a renowned journalist who was shot by the communists the day Tirana was liberated from the Germans. My grandmother did everything to protect her children and save them from a life of persecution and deprivation. She denounced her husband even though she knew he had been innocent. She worked and showed devotion to the communists although deep inside she hated them for what they had done to her family. And she brought up children that had to

35

be survivors. Although venerated by the system, my father always felt he was an outsider. Even at the top of his game, he was paranoid and doubtful, even when his music was celebrating the glory of the regime and its leader Enver Hoxha, he reserved inside him the shadow of disbelief in a system that essentially, had killed his chance for having a father and a complete life.

I never knew this about my father, he never spoke about it. Only this year I found out to what extent his past haunted him. For over 50 years, without raising the suspicions of the state, he had carefully collected information about his father and the circumstances of his death. After the collapse of communism, he had spent thousands of hours in the state's archives trying to piece together his father's story. I felt very ashamed to find out, only this year, that his greatest ambition for the past 10 years had been to reinstate his father as a hero. He confessed to me the agony and despair at the prospect of leaving this life without bringing some justice to him. And he finally succeeded, in 2018 my grandfather has been finally declared a Hero of the Second World War.

I could hear all the longing in my father's music. His soul could only be free and expressive in his music. In Elgar, I feel the same power of expression, that complete openness of feelings, direct communication and power that goes straight to the soul with no waste.

Soon after I arrived inside the rehearsal room the orchestra stopped playing and everybody went out for a break. As I opened the violin case and started tuning a thought went through my mind. Maybe things don't necessarily connect, it is us that make the connection, between things we love, things we long for, and we find mysterious threads to connect the dots. After all, how can Elgar be relevant in this place? How can his life and experiences make sense in this small and quite claustrophobic environment? He might have felt an outsider, but he was still born in one of the greatest nations and carried in his DNA the pride and glory of the British history. How could he have anything to do with the journey of my father and his music?

This was an important rehearsal, the one in which we had to bring it all together before the performance. I was determined to make them listen to me. The introduction started again loud and hectic and we had to stop a couple of times for the orchestra to make the necessary dynamic changes. The conductor this time was less forgiving and much more demanding. They started feeling the pressure and the level of concentration was much higher. Still, there was always somebody talking or making silly remarks. The lack of work-ethic was evident and that translated in the music. I was determined to play Elgar and not some loud shape of his music. Good music is like a person, it has many layers. Notes and rhythms are just the starting point, the next layer comes with dynamics and timing but the true genius of a work stands in the synergy between the parts, how they relate to each other. Playing chamber music from a very young age builds the ability to connect with the synergy and emerge yourself much deeper in the music, making it a bigger experience. This is what was lacking in this performance, the ability to listen to each other. It reminded me so much of the Albanian parliament. If you happen to listen to a session of the parliament or a public debate you are very quickly shocked by the lack of any understanding between the parties. Everybody seems to speak simultaneously, sometimes saying the same thing in different forms, and nobody listens. Nobody accepts anybody else's opinion because nobody has the patience to listen. As a result, I often felt people lived in their little boxes talking inside out without having the ability to breathe anything in. The only person I felt had the ability to listen was my mother, the humblest of all people I have met, the quietest, and the wisest. She is silent in a place of noise, it must be so difficult to be her, absorbing all that cacophony and yet still finding the strength to love people, even the ones with the greatest flaws.

When I got to the second Windflower theme I played the softest *Pianissimo* imaginable, wanting to make them experience solitude. I was quite happy with the result, I think I managed an almost *Piano* from the orchestra and felt them shaking a little. All that loud sound, maybe it is just a facade, a wall against the outside world, to protect themselves from being exposed and from having to listen to those inner thoughts. We were finally embracing Elgar and the music was bending and moving more organically.

How much of this music did they get? Everybody I spoke to was trying to compare Elgar's music with another composer. Somebody compared it to Brahms, another to Wagner and Strauss. I couldn't agree with them. I didn't want to label Elgar, it is not fair to do that with anybody.

(Track 4 - First Movement - Development)
https://aldadizdari.co.uk/elgartracks/track-4/

The next morning I made my way to the University of Arts' Concert Hall. It is the only decent concert hall we have in Albania, built by the Italians in the 30s. The hall has excellent acoustics and is intimate and elegant. But it is always cold and the backstage is almost in ruins. It shows the state of the arts and the efforts to promote it in post-communist Albania and the transitional years. I do not know why we continue to say *transitional* as it has been almost 27 years since the fall of communism, but Albania continuous to be in a perpetual transitional state.

We had a general rehearsal in an icy cold hall with most of the musicians wearing their coats. The wind players were struggling to keep their instruments in tune and nobody wanted to rehearse for very long, considering a general rehearsal just a run through of the repertoire. I was slightly irritated by the idea that although so much effort had been expended by all parties to make this premiere happen, we still had no confirmation of any British authorities attending the performance. On the same evening, since this was the 28th of November, our National Independence Day, the President of Albania was hosting a big dinner for all the dignitaries and so many of the influential supporters of my father's music and those cultured enough to appreciate the significance of this moment were unable to attend the concert. So again, my quiet and wise mother had been right. In my romantic euphoria, she had had the foresight to envisage this.

Despite all the general neglect for what I thought to be an important premiere in the cultural life of Albania, at 6.30pm the bus of the national TV arrived with three cameras to record the performance. This immediately lifted my spirit and made me look forward even more to the performance. My Edwardian dress transported me to a spot in Queen's Hall in London (which was unfortunately destroyed by bombing in 1941), where this concert would have normally taken place during Elgar's lifetime and, while waiting in the horrible little room at the back of the stage down some very dangerous and wobbly stairs, my heart was again warmed by the melodies and the sounds of my father's symphony opening the evening's performance. I was fully aware this was a very special moment. My parents were still alive, my father was in the audience listening to his work some 40 years after he had written it and I was going to perform Elgar's Violin Concerto for the first time in Albania more than 100 years after it was written. It was a memory I was going to cherish for years to come. When my parents are no longer here, the memory of that evening, of the emotions, of everything they sacrificed for me, of everything they lived through, of all the fears they must have felt, of all the love they managed to give us in the midst of darkness and all the beautiful feelings they decided to share through music will only become more precious. I felt humbled by the magnitude of that moment. Faced with the scale of my emotions that evening all the other hiccups and all the other provincial let downs felt tiny and immeasurable. Dreams are not made out of grand gestures, they don't need recognition from the outside world. You feel it in your bones when dreams come to life when you see them form a reality. For me, Elgar in Albania, on the National Day of Albania, was a dream come true.

...

The following morning came like a beam of sunshine in the brightest of skies. I almost screamed and melted with love for Albania and my soul, still lifted in some divine musical dimension, was shimmering in the lightest and brightest states of being. I couldn't wait to get out on the streets and love my city and in my shy and silent way tell it how much I loved and missed it. Everything, from my excited state of mind to the streets and the weather reminded me of my childhood, of those days of national celebration which young children can so easily be part of. The streets were decorated with flags and national symbols. The big boulevard had been turned into a pedestrian area with wooden huts and stands selling memorabilia and local produce. In one spot there was a stand with an army brass band performing military marches, on another stage local children from the music schools were performing a little concert and everywhere you could see girls dressed in Albanian traditional costumes. I hadn't seen those costumes since I was a small child. During communism our biggest cultural event was a National Folk Festival where groups from all regions of Albania participated, dressed in their special costumes, performing music from their region. Back then, at the age of probably 3 or 4, I must have thought Albania was probably the largest country in Europe, judging by 30 or more national costumes in all colours and shapes and the music that varied so much from region to region. The festival took place in the birthplace of our leader, Enver Hoxha, a city called Gjirokastra, with such interesting architecture, now a Unesco World Heritage Site. The city is also the birthplace of our most beloved and world-renowned author Ismail Kadare who made his city immortal in his book "Chronicle in Stone". It is my favourite Albanian book for the simple reason that it captures that vision I had of Albania as a child, a great country of eagles, much larger than the territory it contains, with a history that spreads for thousands of years and a language that is as old as ancient Greek, a country of extreme beauty and contrast, inhabited by strong people who are vibrant survivors of the greatest historical dramas.

Albania, like a little time capsule, sucked me in again, as it did every time, into a different dimension. In four days I was again transformed by this country that holds my roots, that are a little too raw, sometimes painful, other times filled with exaltation, but never, ever boring or placid. It took me less than 4 days to go back to feeling an extension of this land that I judge and sometimes loathe, that frustrates me no end with its inability to get a grip of its own fate, and those people with faces that tell a thousand stories and still smile with beaming eyes that can't seem to find their freedom or peace but, despite it all, love and live life to the fullest. Never did I feel the sunshine so powerfully on me and the sky's blue so brightly above me. And I fell in love again and again, with a mountain called Dajti, that sits above the capital, like an old man by the fire, stirring the fates of his little people down below.

I was far away from the Malvern Hills that inspired Elgar, the soft rolling hills that held the secret of his music and his melodies. But I could understand his love for those hills and for his beloved England. His quiet sensitivity that burnt so deeply and so powerfully in his music. I am sure that even if the musicians and audiences in this place couldn't capture all his meaning and musical world, they could feel the love and sincerity in the writing and for a few moments in the lengthy work that is the violin concerto, they listened, to themselves, to each other and made peace with the world and found a balance that could only take place in music.

The author and conductor, Alexander Walker, in an art
nouveau-style cafe in Oradea.

Chapter 3

Elgar in Oradea - Romania- February 2016

We arrived at the Cluj International Airport on a very cold February morning. Cluj is the third largest city in Romania, and the largest in the heart of Transylvania with a mixed population of Romanians, Hungarians, Germans and Jews who create a rich cultural and political fabric.

As I came out of the airport and made my way to the taxi rank I couldn't help thinking about those early days in Romania and my memories of this city. I didn't have much time to explore but hoped I could spend a little time on my way back from Oradea. I was heading for the coach station to catch a bus to Oradea some three hours away, my next destination. As I sat in the back of a taxi I asked the driver about the state of affairs in Cluj. Taxi drivers are the best people to give you the pulse of a city. Before I could even finish my question the reply was rolling continuously: 'The politics in this country are ruining everything. These people, they are all corrupt politicians, they are selling the country to the Hungarians. This is Romania, this is the land of the Daci. There is no place for Hungarians here. We are working for them, ending up serving them. This never happened during Ceausescu. He knew how to handle the Hungarians. We had our pride, we had our land. Now we have nothing'. He carried on and on without stopping until we reached the coach station, an old and derelict building with gates for different coaches with the destination written at the front of the bus. I was quite relieved to leave the taxi. It was freezing cold, and the cold took me back to those first months of my life as a young teenager in Romania.

I had never been so cold in my entire life. In Bucharest, by the end of November, the snow had covered the streets and the temperatures had dropped to minus 10. I didn't have the appropriate clothes for these temperatures. I had a long black woollen coat that went all the way to the ground and wore many layers of jumpers underneath. But because the coat was made of wool, it got wet in the snow and it was so hard to walk. The snow sometimes reached up to the hips and we all walked in the trail made in the snow. I would make my way to the trolleybus and to reward myself for this misery I would stop at the corner cafeteria and treat myself to two cakes. This was my daily routine which I didn't skip even when the weather got better. I had never tasted such delicious cakes before. In Albania, we only had limited supplies of sugar or butter. In the years before I left the shops in Albania were completely empty, sometimes you went with money and there was nothing to buy. Coming to Romania was a huge improvement where eating was concerned. The food supplies were plentiful and the variety of products pretty much unparalleled. In Romania they had food markets in every district, they had indoor supermarkets with foreign produce. I couldn't understand them complaining about things and how life was when where I came from was far worse. Back then I wasn't aware I came from the poorest country in Eastern Europe. Everything else was an improvement. The cafeterias on every corner had many varieties and most cakes were delicious. I soon forgot the cold and what it entailed and focused on the reward and all the new tastes I was able to enjoy.

Those early memories of Romania drew me to the corner

kiosk at the coach station. I was partly hungry and partly curious to check whether some of those old products still existed. I was surprised to find most of them still available. The corn flour puffs I used to love, the little biscuits with cocoa cream in the middle, the cheap Romanian pretzels we used to snack on and the famous coffee powder that made the worst coffee ever. Oh, food can transport you back in time in a flash. I didn't feel like eating any of it but they all brought back memories from those long years I spent in Romania, and so many were connected to those first months after moving there. Was it because I didn't speak the language or because I was lonely and for the first time without the protecting shell of my parents? It felt as if the memories from those early days, although silent, were stronger than the rest.

The bus to Oradea came into the platform and we slowly made our way on board. I went to the back of the bus and put the violin on one of the seats while I took off my coat and put my luggage up in the compartment above. The bus suddenly moved away from the platform knocking the violin case from the seat to the floor. I was mortified. I usually kept the instrument tucked between my legs at all times. It was the safest way not to forget it on a train or bus and make sure it was protected from any shock. I rushed to open it and check. At first glance, it seemed OK. I closed it quickly and placed it firmly between my legs. We were leaving Cluj and heading towards Oradea, the last Romanian city before the border with Hungary.

The bus travelled along a winding road, crossing higher and lower hills. The scenery was beautiful. Everywhere you looked you could see mountains and green. In the background Romanian pop music was playing loudly on the radio. It seemed like time had stood still in this music, it could have been the same song and singer as when I lived there. It is a very specific style, completely artificial with girls who start the song whispering and before you know it, explode in a kind of love hysteria. This music is everywhere, in every bar, every public place. In every Eastern European country, you hear the same song sung in a different language, but they all sound the same, a monotonous rhythm and banal melody. It has no national identity, absolutely no taste and everybody loves it.

The imagery outside was gorgeous, we were travelling through the lower Carpathian Mountains and some of the prettiest parts of Transylvania, a place I hope everybody can visit one day because it is such a melting pot of cultures, traditions and simply, life.

After a couple of hours of travelling through woods and hills that reminded me a lot of the Malvern Hills, accompanied by the worst music in the world, we entered the outskirts of the city. The centre had all the characteristics of a sweet little Austro-Hungarian town, beautiful architecture, run-down buildings, a river and the Continental Hotel where we were to stay.

The hotel was what we called during communism times a High Riser, as it was the highest building in the centre. It was situated by the bank of a river and had a panoramic view of the city's square.

I rushed into the room and the first thing I couldn't wait to do was inspect my violin. I discovered that on the impact the screws from the handle of the case had made a little hole in the rib of the instrument, nothing much but enough to send me into a total panic. I called specialists and friends, frantically sending pictures to them to establish the damage. The violin sounded ok, a little shaken, like an old lady knocked over by a bicycle. I spent the rest of the evening making sure I could play with it the next day.

In the morning I decided to walk to the Philharmonic Hall which is located in the old city, next to the National Opera and the pedestrian area. This small town on the border between Hungary and Romania has a population that is fairly mixed, hence the language spoken in most institutions is both Romanian and Magyar (Hungarian). The city used to have a rich cultural life and was very much influenced by the Austria-Hungarian Empire with most of the musicians in the orchestra travelling from Vienna or Prague. I was looking forward to performing with an orchestra that had its roots in a tradition started in the 18th century by the youngest brother of Haydn, Johann Michael Haydn and later under the patronage of Maria Theresa of Austria.

I was going to perform with the same conductor as in Oxford and Albania, and it was such a lovely feeling, we were growing to know each other so well through this piece. I liked his understanding and we shared a lot of insightful conversations about the writing and the content of the piece. He had promoted Elgar's works in Eastern Europe for much longer than I and had given many orchestras the opportunity to get to know Elgar in depth, with instructions from somebody who had studied and had a clear affinity with the music.

As I entered the concert hall I was greeted by the sounds of the Introduction and Allegro for Strings by Elgar; the warm and lovely sounds made me joyful and happy. The hall was intimate, a little dry acoustically but small enough not to be a problem.

I had the best feelings so far. The orchestra sounded good. They were a calm group, concentrated and well behaved. They respected the conductor and worked really hard to improve. In the interval, the wind players remained to practice rather than going out to smoke. I could see the clear difference between what I had experienced before and them. The professionalism was an indication of the standard we could expect in this performance and I immediately felt the pressure to do my best. The concerto felt still young in my hands.

The first rehearsal was spent mainly playing through and working on certain areas, especially in the third movement. To many performers, this movement seems really long, challenging technically and a nightmare for memorisation. It starts with the violin part bubbling around arpeggios that rise up to form harmonic peaks and the whole passage grows into a recitativo theme that has all the virtuosic features of a romantic concerto. Despite the level of difficulty, the passages feel natural for the performer. It is a testament to Elgar's understanding and his abilities with the violin. He not only loved the instrument and explored to the fullest its singing qualities, he managed to create a comfortable part for the soloist that, despite the length and complexity, feels enjoyable when performing. His close friendship with the leader of London Symphony Orchestra, W.H. (Billy) Reed had been very fruitful for the concerto. Billy made many suggestions and it was in the hours he spent with Elgar, playing the concerto, which was hung in sheets from every corner of the room, that Elgar made many additions to the violin part, added much more colour and came up with some truly memorable ideas that make this concerto unique *.
(Track 5 - First Movement - Development)
https://aldadizdari.co.uk/elgartracks/track-5/

I tried to keep all the fingering suggested by Elgar, his particular choice of colour and timbre. In all the movements he sometimes prefers some big or eccentric leaps into the G string rather than a change of string. To me, those are clear decisions that have a direct connection with the mood of the passage or the sound effect. Although they are tricky to nail, as the entire arm has to twist upwards, as well as a nightmare for the intonation, I wouldn't change anything.

…

We spent quite a long time on the lengthy Cadenza just before the coda in the third movement. The conductor tried to get the orchestra to create the right sound with their pizzicato tremolos and the amazing chords held by the horns at the end of the phrases. As the solo violin plays the main leitmotivs, featuring mainly the Windflower themes and flourishes them with virtuosic passages, the orchestra is engaged in creating a sound world that enriches the violin part without detracting from the main themes, just enhancing them with a sound effect that concludes with the chords in the horns. It is the most emotional place in the piece, its heart, and in every performance so far I felt I hadn't captured it. Maybe I would never be able to reach such perfect balance, as the beauty of that moment is such a divine element it seems to be a point that we strive for but can not capture. In the end, it can only reflect the place you are with the piece at that given moment but also with yourself, with the world, it is an all-encompassing experience.

I often thought of Elgar's choice of performer for the premiere of one of his favourite compositions. In 1910 he dedicated his concerto to the great virtuoso violinist, Fritz Kreisler who was not only a performer who embodied perfectly the great Viennese tradition, but who was also a good composer himself. He had the ability to delve deeper into the musical meaning of the piece while having all the technical facilities needed to tackle such a monumental work. He ensured the work was focused more on the emotional connection than on the exhibition of virtuosity.

(Track 6 - First Movement - Recap)

He was the performer who was described as the "King of the Violin", one that never played very quickly but had a thousand vibratos. Later on, the concerto had another important resurrection, in the hands of a very young virtuoso, Yehudi Menuhin.

We finished a very satisfying rehearsal and I felt better than ever about our coming concert and the possibilities in front of us. The British conductor knew Oradea very well and he wanted to show me some corners of this city that inspired him the most. We walked through the main square and headed for the pedestrian area. In the corner of a beautiful Art Nouveau building, we entered his favourite restaurant in town. It was a big hall with ornate cupolas and amazing gilded ceilings and walls adorned with huge vintage mirrors. This place was stunning. It could have been in the centre of old Vienna and I immediately had a feeling I had travelled in time and very shortly I would meet Stefan Zweig or Alban Berg, and in a corner, Freud would be taking notes.

Stefan Zweig was the author that invaded and inspired most of my teenage years back in Albania and the one who made me love everything nostalgic and the world that had vanished with the rise of the Nazis. There was another reason why we loved Zweig back then. His collection of short stories was translated so beautifully in Albanian it almost captured the scent around each story. Zweig, although almost unknown in England, was indeed an important figure in Vienna, connected at the turn of the century to the highest artistic and musical circles there. He described an elegant and vanishing world so well and with such power, that one could not forget the tragic ending of that world and his life. He committed suicide together with his wife after emigrating to South America following the Jewish persecution.

51

His short stories became even dearer to me after reading his final book "The World of Yesterday". But the translation of his work into Albanian was to me the key to his success. I couldn't help but think how true that is for music as well. Musicians have such an important mission, we may not be the most creative individuals, but we have in our hands the creations of some brilliant minds, and it is down to us to translate them and offer them to the world. This is not an aspect mentioned much in the music schools when they teach you the craft, most teachers fail to explain that the mission of the performer is, first and foremost, to the music, not just to themselves.

We sat down and almost simultaneously talked about the evocative feelings this place arose in us. They were exactly the same. At present Oradea was famous for its shoe-making factories. Most of the Italian shoes were actually made in this place and exported around the world. In the past, it must have been much more than that. Judging by this café, at some point, this town must have been at the heart of an important empire and filled with interesting people who were used to the best. They would have spent their time going to the opera and following concerts in the Philharmonic Hall. I had a feeling people around here preferred to speak Hungarian to Romanian as often I couldn't understand what they were talking about and had difficulty realising we were still in Romanian territory. The politics there had always been tricky with many territories continuously changing hands between the Hungarians and the Romanians. The religious landscape made things even more complicated. Romania is almost entirely an Orthodox country and the Hungarians are predominately Calvinist or Catholic.

We decided to walk to the hotel following the bank of the river and enjoying the beautiful architecture. I loved this place. I was faced again by the old world of the turn of the century, but a glorious past that gave much stimulation to my imagination. It reminded me of many books I had read in high school years when I was studying for the Romanian Literature A Levels. Not only had I joined the high school halfway through, not knowing the language, I had to fit in with the school's curriculum which included subjects like Romanian Literature and Romanian History. I am so grateful for those years now but back then I was not so happy as the workload was impossible. I made a decision to aim as low as possible and just try to pass the exams as best as I could. I had to work enough to pass these exams with dignity, my pride was important to me. As I faced the prospect of having to read and prepare some 60 books in Romanian in the space of around 2 months, negative thoughts of failure were continuously present. In those days I used to live in the students' accommodation in Bucharest surrounded by people much older than myself. I looked for a literature major student and came across a very kind girl who gave me the first ray of hope. She decided to help me prepare for the exam. As the time was limited and I couldn't read everything I needed to, we focused on those essential books to be covered and then she filled in the gaps by giving me a resumé for most of the others. And that is how I fell in love with the Romanian literature and got to know this country through their books. I got to know a Romania beyond the grip of communism back in a period that felt much freer and more prosperous. Romania had once been an important European player, with a monarchy connected to the biggest European royalties and a history that had had periods of glory and failure. I got to know a Romania that was very rich in natural resources and a land so vast it had boundless prospects of agricultural development. Romania had produced some of the greatest thinkers of our times such as Ionesco, Eliade and Cioran and some of the most influential European artists and musicians such as Enescu, Lipati and Brancusi. This was not a country at the edge of Europe, but a central point of European culture. It was during those stressful afternoons spent in the little room of my student friend that I discovered the real Romania, the one I loved so much and received such inspiration from. The nostalgia of those days grew in me while walking in the parks of Oradea. I had never been here before but through the literature, I had already seen its past and its glory and I felt the love this place had already bestowed on me, many years ago.

One of the special elements of this journey around these places I had not seen before was the feeling that somehow I knew them already. In some hidden place in my mind, I had captured their essence, their taste and their beauty. Now I was just seeing them with my open eyes, but inside of me I had visited this old world and inhabited it in the shape of a book or a thought taken from some author I came to know and love in those early days in Romania.

…

The next morning we had a press conference to present the programme for the evening. Everything was well organised. We met the director of the Philharmonic Orchestra, a kind man who took his role very seriously and tried his best to give the orchestra a vision and image that went beyond the city's limitations. Everybody impressed me. I wish there could be such a professional attitude in Tirana. All the musicians were rehearsing and warming up. It was a working environment. I don't know whether this was because of the legacy of the place, or because of the mixed roots of the people. One thing was obvious, it didn't feel Eastern European, tired, depressed, poor and desperate. This felt like a thriving community, filled with life and aspirations, and a clear sense of purpose and commitment to its mission.

I liked Oradea, very much. This was a place I would recommend to friends and happily visit again.

Everything felt positive and the concert brought indeed some very good results. Elgar didn't feel far away. He was present. I think it would have reminded him of Vienna and other places that he loved. It had the kind of energy that would have inspired him and he would have certainly loved the spas around Oradea.

In the evening the concert hall was full and the crowd was very enthusiastic. We created a good balance and the orchestra felt integrated with the soloist, the dialogue was organic, with the right mix of diversity and intimacy. My instinct had been right all along. There was an innate understanding of this piece and Elgar felt completely absorbed and accepted here. It was such an exhilarating performance and on so many levels more special than it would have been to an audience who knew Elgar and loved his music. Our mission of bringing his music to the furthest parts of Eastern Europe was coming to a climax.

(Track 7 - First Movement - Coda)

https://aldadizdari.co.uk/elgartracks/track-7/

The evening closed with a superb meal near the pedestrian area, a very sophisticated dinner that we had for a fraction of the price it would have cost us in London. I wished I could have had a few more days in Oradea. It seemed like a place well worth extra time exploring.

The next morning I took the coach back to Cluj and by midday was walking around its old streets, tasting Romanian dishes I longed to eat again, such as the famous tripe soup and the stuffed cabbage leaves, things I could only have here.

During my student years in Romania, I found Cluj one of the most interesting places in the country. It was civilised, occidental, cultured and it had very little of that communist feel that most cities in Eastern Europe had. I visited it for the first time just a few months after arriving in the country. Thanks to my violin skills, I was able to integrate into the musical life way before I could communicate properly. I remember those days so clearly. Just a few months after starting my studies at the George Enescu High School in Bucharest, sitting through hours and hours of lectures without understanding a word, just looking at faces and smiling politely at everybody. I learnt quickly how to read faces and distinguish the nice people from not such nice ones. In those early days, just after the revolution, I was the only foreigner in the school and as such, I was immediately seen as an exotic object. Most of my classmates were very friendly in those days because they found in me a good way to practice their English. I was quickly exposed to the different groups in the classroom and dragged around as if to make sure I could make the right choice, eventually. During the break, I was taken to the little café behind the school where the cool kids gathered to smoke. They were mostly boys from privileged backgrounds, surrounded by girls that in American teen movies would be the cheerleaders. The boys were too cool to pay me any attention and most of the time waited for the girls to make their seductive moves around them. In every break, they were enveloped in their own little world of outdoing each other and competing on who was the coolest and looked the trendiest. I realised very quickly this was not my crowd and they certainly didn't miss my quiet and smoke-free presence in their breaks. I then joined the group of geeks that didn't leave the classroom during the break, instead, they spoke about very boring subjects and practised their basic English with me. In return they offered very generously their time to help me with my Romanian and were very helpful later on when we had to take tests, sharing information and helping me copy. I am not proud of that, but in those days the only way forward was by copying. A very strict History teacher demanded in less than two months that I stand up in front of the class and speak about a subject, otherwise, he would fail me for that term. I was determined to pass and my geeky friends came to my rescue. One particular girl, with an encyclopaedic mind, took me under her wing and made it her life mission to teach me one lesson in Romanian so I could stand in front of the class and recite it. I picked the only subject that made sense vaguely to me, the story of Vlad the Impaler, known to the world as Dracula. After days of learning the words like a parrot, I went in front of the class and passed my test in history. As my first months in high school passed going from lesson to lesson taught in a strange language which I couldn't understand, feeling homesick to the point of despair, there was only one way forward. The only language in which I could communicate with these people was music. I spent every moment practising, desperately trying to find some common ground and be accepted by them. I joined the high school in October and by the end of November, I had to perform in the technical examination on the violin. I passed that so successfully that I was given the highest mark in my year. This was my attempt to fit in, instead, it made me an instant enemy. As soon as the results came out I was immediately ostracised. I was no longer the exotic foreigner they practised English with, I was the competition. From then on there were no more friendly faces and people were not inviting me to join their groups. I sat on my own on a bench for most of the rest of the semester and the only person who continued to give me some support was the geeky girl with long hair and big glasses. Boy, high school can be tough! It is as if you wake up as a toddler, surrounded by love and attention and then suddenly you are thrown to the lions to see whether you can make it or not. Since I didn't see any other way out, I embraced my solitude and played my violin non-stop. Which is how I managed to make it to the National Olympiads which that year took place in the city of Cluj. It was obvious that pain brought great progress because my lack of language communication was bringing great musical results and I remember that by the end of that term I had won most of the internal competitions and pre-selections to the

National Olympiads. They were the most prestigious national competitions in Romania open in all subjects. Every high school had a limited number of participants and we all competed internally until the right number was reached. I made it to the third round and was excited to be able to compete nationally until I was told I couldn't. As I entered my teacher's studio that day I could see her face really crinkled with anger, which was a surprise to me as she was the calmest and most distant person I had ever come across. She was a welcoming figure of balance in those hectic days in my life and in some strange ways I liked her distance and her emotional coolness. That day she was not calm though and as soon as I entered the class she started to explain how they had received anonymous calls regarding my participation in the national olympiad being illegitimate. After all, I was not Romanian and I was taking the place of another deserving student. I could understand their point, but why had they left me to participate in the selections internally? Why had they given me hope in the first place? That was the reason my teacher was so angry, to the point I could feel her fake curls almost straighten with tension. She then asked me to go to the Ministry of Education and speak to somebody in charge to ask them to find a solution.

There I was, with hardly any language skills, making my way purposefully to the ministry, with an important mission at hand. When I entered the ministry I was not so sure about my mission anymore. I felt such a lonely and lost person, thousands of miles from any protection or love, completely lost in this city. I knocked very shyly on one of the doors and asked to see the only man I knew there, the person in charge of the foreign students' affairs, Mr Teodorescu. He had interviewed me before giving me the student scholarship to study in Romania and I had received very warm and kind vibes from him. He came out and met me in the hallway and invited me to his office. I had no idea whether there was any point to make but I explained the best I could the situation and in my broken Romanian, I was able to share my feelings of injustice. He smiled gently and left the room for a few minutes which seemed interminable to me. When he returned he was accompanied by a lady. She was loud and bossy and seemed completely in control of everything. She could have been the minister as far as I could gather because she debated with Mr Teodorescu in the most direct and almost patronising way. In the beginning, she started by saying that the places were limited and that indeed there was no place for foreigners to participate in a National Olympiad. But when Mr Teodorescu pleaded on my behalf, she hesitated a moment and gave me a quick look. At this point, I was ready and quite happy to give up the battle. But, as if by magic, and a moment of inspiration, she turned to him and said: 'I know what we shall do. We shall give an extra place to the school so that Alda can compete'. And that was how I got to travel to Cluj and represent my high school in the National Olympiads. I have to say, I was not more popular after that move, quite the opposite. Now, not only had I to sit on my own in pretty much all subjects, sometimes I had to endure comments like "Alda has friends in the Ministry". There are some advantages to not speaking the language so well, a lot of it can sound like noise and in those days only music made sense anyway.

I loved Cluj. It felt such a different city from Bucharest, far more genuine and jolly. I related much better to it because it had the dimensions of Tirana, smaller and more compact. We rehearsed in the music conservatoire which had a great tradition and in the competition I was judged by one of the great soloists of Romania that in his heyday had won the famous Tchaikovsky Competition. I loved the architecture and almost wished I was studying there rather than Bucharest.

...

On that cold evening in February 2016 I left Cluj filled with a rich experience of music, food and memories. They all seemed sweet and dear. I didn't feel depressed leaving as I knew I would be returning again in a few months for another performance of Elgar, in another unknown place in a country I had called home for a while.

Philharmonic Hall in Bacau.

Chapter 4

Elgar in Bacau - Moldavia - October 2016

The bus station was a concrete structure, with a little kiosk at the entrance, but no sign for the station. Crowds of shabby people rushed for a bus or waited patiently for one. The faces looked sad, tired, with very little sign of peace. As the buses approached the gate the passengers silently made their way to the respective gates. I followed the group gathering at Terminal 1 where buses to Bacau parked. I had left London only 5 hours ago but as I stood there I could have been a hundred years and million miles away. Nothing was familiar yet at the same time, in a distant time, it was. The concrete building and the graffiti on the wall were reminders of my past. The buildings around the station, tired communist architecture, typical of all Eastern Europe, could have been from the city of my birth. This feeling of strange yet familiar made me focus on the faces of the people at the station. The faces told a thousand stories as if taken from a Dostoyevsky novel. Most people had, to say the least, damaged teeth. They were badly dressed in old jackets and some even had hats dating from the 19th century. Some young girls were wearing very tight jeans and too much makeup. Nobody smiled. As we loaded onto the bus, I moved toward the middle and took a seat by the window, the violin firmly between my legs. The air was soon filled with the smell of sausages and salami, onion and boiled eggs. The smells took me back to my childhood, on the crowded trains that took us from Tirana to the holiday resort in Pogradec in the South Eastern region by lake Ohrid. I never made it to the train through the doors, I was always pushed through the window before the doors opened, to secure as quickly as possible places to sit for the long journey. The trains were very full and very slow. It usually took 7 hours and we all had packed lunches very similar to those I was smelling today. I remember being so excited and happy that I didn't mind the hardship. Soon I was going to be at my grandparents' home. My maternal grandma would open the door of the wardrobe and there, at the bottom of the shelf she would have stored around 20 jars of homemade jams, the most delicious jams I had ever tasted. By the end of our stay, there would be nothing left. But she was happy to see the jars empty, it gave her a reason to start the next batch. In that simple apartment by Lake Ohrid, with no fridge, washing machine or warm water, I experienced for the first time a feeling of complete happiness and freedom, the kind of love only grandparents can give you because they know much more about life than your parents and have more time to give you.

...

We left the bus station of Iasi (the capital of the Moldavian Region) and headed towards Bacau, a place I had never seen before, not even on a map. I had heard a lot about Iasi because of the great musicians who came from there. The wonderful Romanian composer George Enescu had a great influence on the musical life of Iasi. He was born in Moldavia and helped transform Romania into a cultural centre with progressive thinking that had much more in common with the great western tradition than the Russian influence in the region. But Bacau, although in Moldavia, really didn't mean anything to me. As the bus advanced through the Romanian countryside I looked out the window at the landscape that surrounded us, flat countryside, brown land, some agricultural but mainly plain undeveloped land with a lot of empty distribution centres scattered around that gave me a sense of loneliness. Why did this landscape remind me of Chekhov and Gogol's short stories?

Was it the vast land, the endless horizon, the sense of being lost in time?

Whenever we encountered a little town it was the same scene of derelict concrete communist buildings with badly lit tired facades. After two hours of driving, we approached the city of Bacau. I left the bus and made my way to the taxi rank. I boarded an old Dacia, probably older than myself. I wondered if the brakes worked. Inside I was touched by the clean covers, they were almost like the blankets people used during communism to cover their sofas and make them warmer during the winter. The driver had a face full of pain but was very polite and gallant. I could tell from those clean covers and his car that he was a man with dignity. His life had started and would probably finish in this place, but there was pride in his existence. He was not a victim. He didn't try to overcharge me or pretend he didn't have change like many drivers in Bucharest would. He charged me very little and gave me the correct change. I had met my first person in Bacau and I liked what I saw.

The hotel was a tall grey building, another typical communist building in the centre of the city. Most of them are called Continental Hotel, in the hope, the name will give some international prestige to the place. Inside it was as if I was walking back 40 years, with tired carpets on the floor, wooden panels on the walls and very dim lights everywhere. I made my way to the room which overlooked a complex of buildings from the same period as the hotel. The original colours of the buildings had been washed away and now they all looked grey. The balconies had been customised differently for every apartment, some had been covered by glass or turned into storage rooms. It made the buildings look irregular and distorted.

I closed the curtain and opened my luggage. After all, I was here on business, there was a job to be done. I called the room of the conductor and a voice responded in a mixture of Romanian and Italian. He wanted to see me for a short rehearsal that same evening. After a long journey of over 10 hours, my hands felt quite sore and the circulation was slow. I quickly opened my violin and started warming up. There is nothing worse than playing with cold muscles. You can easily hurt your tendons. I tried to get my muscles pumping some blood as soon as possible. Shortly after, I met the conductor, a middle-aged elegant Italian, in the foyer of the hotel and we walked out into the fresh evening air. The concert hall was only a few hundred meters away and the main hall was free. The building was not large and from the outside looked ugly but inside the hall was intimate. I made my way to the stage and started the rehearsal. I played through the concerto, with him humming the orchestral part which was quite disturbing at times. My hands felt puffed and numb, the shifting felt heavy and my bow felt like a giant lorry trying to make a quick turn. I played through to the end and I thought he looked relieved. He said it was going to be easy. I asked him what he meant and he replied: 'The last time I played this piece it was in Russia and it was a nightmare. The violinist was taking all sorts of liberties with the music and it was extremely hard to keep up with her'. I explained that this was completely against my beliefs. With any piece of music, I try to put myself in the position of a translator of the text and not the creator of it. I would certainly not be able to come up with something more interesting than Brahms, Beethoven or Elgar. For me, the score is like the Bible. You keep reading the Bible and every day it might make you think of different things and you might interpret certain events in different ways but at the end you are just reading the Bible, not creating it. Well, I am not sure my comparison stacks up as, come to think about it, in the name of the Bible and ways it has been interpreted, wars have been fought, worlds have been lost and people have suffered. I only made this comparison because I have always believed my religion was music, the only thing that seems like a centre of existence to me and the only thing that makes me contemplate a sort of God. After all, it is very difficult to imagine a work like Bach's Ciaccona without contemplating the existence of a higher order.

Respecting the score can sometimes be a daunting experience, sometimes it can be an almost impossible task. But for me, the more challenging the set of directions the more interesting the score becomes because the music starts to take shape and rather than you playing the music you start being the music. The score of Elgar's Violin Concerto is full of notation, very detailed dynamics and tempo changes. There is a big dramatic arch and within that are smaller arches. I discovered very early on working on this piece that Elgar, like many exceptional composers, knows exactly what to write and why. He doesn't leave any notation to chance. Everything written on the score represents a specific colour or nuance he wants to project. Throughout the piece, there is a continuous dialogue between the solo violin and the orchestra and especially different solo instruments in the wind section. The leitmotivs travel from instrument to instrument and are weaved through and developed seamlessly.

After a quick chat, we made our way back to the hotel. I went straight to bed and forgot all about the place I was in, the buildings, the mood. All I was thinking about was Elgar and my painful hands. I needed a good night's sleep. I had my first rehearsal with the orchestra the following day.

It was a grey morning and it had started to rain. I didn't like the rain, it made me melancholic. I had slept well and my hands felt much better. I went downstairs for breakfast. The foyer was almost empty. This was indeed a sad place. The coffee was undrinkable and I decided to go for a green tea instead and some eggs and local ham and cheese. I went back to my room and started warming up for the rehearsal at 11.30.

When I arrived at the Philharmonic hall I found most of the musicians outside smoking. This was the scene in every philharmonic orchestra in Eastern Europe. The pause means cigarettes, everybody smokes. All over the world musicians are not the healthiest individuals, cigarettes or alcohol, sometimes both, go with the territory.

I went in and started to feel excited and scared about what I was about to do.

It doesn't matter how many times you play a piece, every concert is a new journey, every rehearsal comes with a new set of rules and resolutions and you just gather the information that your body is sending you and you make a plan for the next rehearsal or performance, and you know that some things will work and some won't.

The orchestra took a while to settle down. Another feature of the Eastern European orchestras, pauses are usually at least 5 minutes longer than agreed. Finally, we were all on stage, ready to start this piece, for them the first performance, for me a long journey that had started a few years back with an original score with markings by Henry Wood.

Everything felt loud and a little coarse but at least they were following the conductor and I liked his knowledge. He was clear and followed the score, although at times it felt a little stiff. The problem with detailed scoring is that sometimes the translation can be very literal and maybe the reactions a little artificial. For example, when the score says accelerando, most conductors translate it as faster and there is this sudden change of tempo which I think in many ways doesn't work with Elgar as his accelerandos are always organic and completely fluid, they follow the course of his musical ideas which to my mind work perfectly. He meticulously notated the score to create a very clear vision of the piece but if you don't spend time capturing the emotional context, what it means, how it all connects, you may finish just as lost as if you disregarded his notation.

One of the greatest pleasures of coming back to this piece is that after months of not performing it with an orchestra you forget a little the magnitude of the work, especially the power and the depth you get from the brass section, with the beautiful lines and some of their virtuosic passages. And when you start playing the piece in the first rehearsal you always have again this wondrous moment of discovery, this moment of magic. It doesn't matter how far from home you are, how brutal the architecture is around you, how painful and tired the faces are, how badly musicians are paid. When you start playing this music everything else ceases to exist. You need so much power of concentration, so much strength and stamina you get lost in the music. You are surrounded by an incredible sound world. You don't feel alone or scared. You feel sometimes nostalgia, sometimes joy and electrifying energy. Other times you contemplate a beautiful melody that is so fragile you are scared of crushing it with too much sound or too much vibrato. Nothing is over the top or cheap, the music has so much dignity and nobility, it makes any place more humane. I sincerely believe it makes the audience and performers happier too. Nowadays there is a lost sense of space and time which explains also the faster and faster recordings of this piece. I have to turn to old LPs to find the feeling and spaciousness of a slower pace of life.

I was completely immersed in those feelings and couldn't

help but wonder whether my colleagues could capture the immensity of this moment. Were they feeling what I was feeling? I have always been fascinated by the question of familiarity. Do we appreciate a piece more the more time we spend on it? This is certainly true of pop music. Ordinary tunes are repeated on the radio to the point they become familiar and associated with our personal time, therefore they enter our life and become an important component in our individual story. We like the familiarity those tunes offer and as a result, sometimes quite banal tunes become much loved and cherished. They often remind us of precious moments or people, sometimes they remind us even of a specific street, event or smell.

Is the same true for a classical music piece? Could these musicians understand Elgar, his music and his world?

The rehearsal finished. It went relatively well, thanks to my accurate conductor who guided them through even though at times the dynamic range was coarse and aggressive. So much more to be done but for the moment I was happy. I had had the chance of entering one more time this world and nothing could make me happier.

I rushed back to the hotel with a renewed sense of purpose. I had so much more to do on passages, nuances, sound. I no longer noticed the greyness of the city. I had found my own path, in this strange place, though the poverty was so pronounced and the sadness so acute, I felt completely disconnected and happy. My religion was keeping me purposeful and clearheaded.

Later on that evening, I was thinking about Britishness and what it means to me as a foreigner. For someone travelling as much as I had done all my life from the age of 15, I had come to see people as energetic realms, with either positive or negative radiations. I could feel their energy as soon as I met them, usually from their eyes. I could never understand how some people could be deceived by others as I always felt people on such a strong energetic level that words were almost unnecessary to place them in my map of human behaviour. It was a simple way of melding all the national characteristics into a bigger picture that was not subject to language, religion, or cultural background. These energy levels are similar in many countries, there is roughly a balance of forces that keep us, as a society grounded and functioning. Unless, like myself, you lived through transitional years in a country going through the cruellest, most isolated, communist regime. For many years back in Albania, I felt negativity was much higher than positivity and even when you found positivity, it was sometimes disguised and hidden so deep under layers of frustration, regret and fear that it often came across as negativity until you could understand it and find its truth. In my ever moving world, it was simpler to keep things clean and just divide people into two categories and I rarely thought there were any national characteristics. But it was a very simplistic way of viewing the world. Because people are conditioned by their realities, conditioned by their background, nature, language, exposure and even foods.

Throughout his life, Elgar had a huge admiration for the German tradition. He loved the music that came from Germany, the art, literature; he had a deep sense of connection with their aesthetics and artistic expression. He often felt deeply isolated in England and longed to be part of that great continental tradition. And yet, in so many ways, his isolation made his music even greater and his Britishness even stronger. The fact was he could only write music that was in essence British. But what is Britishness to a foreigner? The truth is, a collective identity made up of every aspect I have encountered with this Britishness is not simple to describe. To me it is a mixture of kindness, nobility, awkwardness, superiority, sense of entitlement, sense of humour, and emotional depth which is hard to read, often coming across as coldness. The perfect example of Britishness I found in W.H.Reed's book about Elgar. After the first rehearsal with Elgar, he had been so impressed by the music that he approached him anxious to know whether he gave harmony or counterpoint lessons. His answer was characteristic; "My dear boy, I don't know anything about those things" *. Britishness is manifested in such complex ways and yet the overall feeling is so clearly visible, from a greasy spoon café to Fortnum & Mason's Food Hall, that sense of quiet pride and clear social place everybody has. Coming from a country that had rid itself of any social scale, where people have no sense of belonging other than in their own family, Britain offers a spectacle in the orderly presentation of classes. From day one I felt included in this country, and yet I still feel a foreigner. I decided after years of living in Britain to make peace with being seen as a foreigner and view it as a positive tool rather than a disadvantage. After all, others, much more accomplished than I, like Joseph Conrad, or Handel were foreigners who embodied Britishness and wrote about it sometimes much better than the British themselves. Maybe even Elgar, the Catholic living in a country of Protestants, felt awkward about his Britishness.

I tried hard that evening, sitting in a hotel room with the worst view in the world, and rain thrashing against the window to capture the idea of Britishness. I went back to Elgar's score to find some short and precise answers. The concerto was written in 1909 -1910, during years of happy fulfilment on all levels for Elgar. The turn of the century finally brought recognition for him, together with some of his finest works including The Enigma Variations, his First Symphony, The Dream of Gerontius, The Apostles, The Violin Concerto followed by the Second Symphony. The Violin Concerto clearly had a muse at its centre, Elgar's close friend, Alice Stuart-Wortley, the daughter of the great painter John Everett Millais. She was one of the most influential ladies at the heart of the artistic circle in London at the time. Elgar wrote the main themes as homage to her and to what she represented in his life. Reading his correspondence with Alice one gets a real sense of who Elgar was as a person. His enormous sensitivity and his feelings of insecurity that bordered on isolation, yet his absolute love for his close friends and the joy he found in them and in places they visited together, come through so vividly. His deep connection with nature and its simplest manifestations gave me my first glimpses of his true Britishness. His main themes in the violin concerto are named the Windflower Themes and in his words, he describes the music, or maybe its muse?

" ...when the east wind rasps over the ground in March and April they merely turn their backs and bow before the squall. They are buffeted and blown, as one may think almost to destruction; but their anchors hold, and the slender-looking stems bend but do not break. And when the rain clouds drive up the petals shut tight into a tiny tent, as country folk tell one, to shelter the little person inside.
*Our native windflower, Anemone nemorosa, is often overlooked by gardeners... Who that has read it can forget Farrer's story of his finding the blue wood-anemone, which, like many another, he had pursued all his life as will-o'-the-wisp? It was in Cornwall, and doubtingly he had plunged into the wood at twilight in search of the phantom flower."**

I fell asleep that night with a vision of the windflowers moving in the wind, with their smiley faces caressed by the sun in the early days of springtime. I was woken up on the morning of the concert with the rain still loud against the window. It was another gloomy, cold morning in the greyest city on earth. The thought of performing Elgar was the only reason I had to be in this place. I had fought very hard in my life to escape the greyness of reality. I had run for so long, sometimes on a very lonely road, and I was back here. This time it had to be different. This time I carried a different light, the light that could make the grey disappear. As I approached the building of the Atheneum I saw the small crowd of musicians taking their daily dose of tobacco. In this grey city, they lived their grey lives with little pride or joy. They didn't often smile and it made me sad. Their lives had not changed much since the fall of the communist system. Most of them drove the same cars, lived in the same apartment blocks and music was just a job they did. Once upon a time, it had been a good life. Being a musician meant you didn't have to wake up at 4 am to work in the chemical plant. Back then being a musician gave you the opportunity maybe to travel abroad and see the world. These days it was a job that paid really badly and made you feel bad about yourself. Not many long to be classical musicians in Eastern Europe anymore.

The programme for the evening was an Elgar Celebration, including a few early works, the Violin Concerto and the Pomp and Circumstance Marches. It was obvious that our Italian conductor had a genuine love of Elgar's music and particularly the Violin Concerto. He had studied the score in great detail and had tried to put his own vision on the work. It was impossible not to notice his national characteristics surfacing a little in his interpretation of the piece. He was a very sensitive man and had captured all the notation in Elgar's score but when it came to the second movement which in the score is marked clearly *Andante Cantabile*, we were always immersed in an almost adagio tempo, from the depth of which it was very difficult to rise. Andante tempo gives an opportunity for the

73

music to flow gently and the emotions not to overwhelm you but fill you with gentle passion and hope, allowing the climaxes to grow without delving into despair. In our current rendition, we were enveloped in such a melancholic mood, everything was taking so much time, and the climaxes were such high mountains we struggled to climb so that when we did we had missed our mission of hope, the music was bordering on self-indulgence. One simple change of tempo would have taken us to the right path, but it was not a path the conductor was easily diverted to. In his true Italian fashion, he was committed to a sweetness of tone and such a mood felt much more like Verdi or Puccini and much less like Elgar.

(Track 8 - Second Movement)

https://aldadizdari.co.uk/elgartracks/track-8/

It was the same in the first movement, my beloved second Windflower theme where the marking is *semplice, a tempo*. Again he was reaching for the climax before we had even started and crawling slowly through the beautiful theme, rather than letting it happen as Elgar so clearly suggested. Again, I thought we were lost in translation, this one was full of pathos before it had a chance to tell the story.

After our general rehearsal, I tried to suggest a few changes in the timings which would have challenged some parts but I knew that in the end, I wouldn't be able to change his long-established interpretation. I just tried to play my part as honestly as possible, keeping my vision intact wherever I felt I had the flexibility.

The concert went generally well. The orchestra was not particularly exciting, the joy was not there and some of the greyness of the city came through in their music making, but they could play and did their part. As could have been predicted from the general rehearsal, the timing left much to be desired, which had a knock-on effect throughout the piece. The concerto felt much longer and heavier and the balance was much harder to strike. I was fully aware of all that, but I learnt that evening to accept it and in my mind, I started running another version of events. I thought about that famous intimate evening in November 1909, when Elgar's closest friends got together to hear the first performance of his violin concerto, in a room with all the lights turned out except for the piano and the violin, Billy Reed on the violin and Elgar on the piano, communicating for the first time to the world the powerful message of this concerto, which celebrates life, love and is full of hope. It must have felt quite different performing this piece after the war, with hope broken and love destroyed for many. It might be the reason why the cello concerto gained so much more momentum, as it explored different kind of moods and emotional states. But isn't the message of music a message of hope? After all, what are we without hope and love?

After the concert, we were invited to a dinner hosted by the director of the philharmonic orchestra with some local influential dignitaries. The dinner took place at the restaurant of our hotel, in the ballroom where half the light bulbs were not working and the place was plunged in semi-darkness. Again the grey feelings returned creeping all over me. About 20 of us were seated around a table and while the waiters were busy bringing out the food various dignitaries started making speeches, interminable speeches that took away my appetite. It was a desperate attempt to show their knowledge of classical music and their cultural depth. One after another they rose to speak. We managed to eat the first course, a mixture of typical Romanian dishes, but as the second course was being served one distinguished member of the academy decided this was the perfect moment to start his humble speech lasting around 40 minutes. I do not remember anything from that speech, not because I couldn't understand, but because I don't think he had any particular theme he was elaborating. During those long moments, I kept looking at the fish which by now had been served some time ago and was slowly going cold. The scene took me back to the seminars I had to endure during my university years in Bucharest. I hated most classes. I generally disliked school mainly because of these lengthy and boring sessions where the lecturers couldn't seem to get to the point but instead would go around and around in circles, constructing a web of words that meant nothing. Bombastic words, the more bombastic the words, the more lost I seemed to get. It all came back. I suddenly felt so sleepy and so tired, the lights seemed to be getting dimmer and dimmer and I was just losing the will to live. Everybody else, except the conductor, seemed quite invigorated by the speech and they kept congratulating the academician for his depth of thinking and his amazing vision about the state of the arts. By then I had just switched off, I couldn't understand Romanian anymore. By the time we had raised our glasses and congratulated him on the speech and everybody was tucking into the cold fish, I had lost my appetite and I just wanted to leave this place. I missed home, I missed London, I missed even the worst airport in England, Luton.

I knew the conductor felt the same way. When we were finally able to leave the party we went for a coffee in the only Italian restaurant in town. We walked out of the hotel and made our way through the little street next to the Atheneum. The rain had finally stopped and it was a pleasant evening. The restaurant was situated in a small house with a courtyard. As soon as we entered we noticed the first big difference, the place was fully lit, it had a homely atmosphere, and people seemed much more upbeat. The music playing was more like the music you hear in London bars and for the first time in three days I was greeted by smiley faces. I smiled back awkwardly as if feeling strange about this new found expression. I ordered a cappuccino and when it arrived it had a message that said *It's Raining Today* and a smiley Emoji. In every city in Eastern Europe, you can find an Italian restaurant and an espresso bar. It doesn't matter how grey and poor the city is, there will always be an Italian willing to prepare coffee and pizza for the population. I always thought that most Italians sooner or later moved to London to start an Italian Café, to import Italian produce and sell it for excruciating prices, to take their revenge on Londoners for doing so much better economically. How wrong I was. If I learnt anything on this journey around Eastern Europe it is that Italians are everywhere. They continue conquering the world with their pizzas and pastas and espresso machines, starting shoemaking and bag making factories. They were even here, in this godforsaken place, bringing some taste, a little sunshine and much-needed kick to the grey depths of Moldavia.

(Edward Elgar "The Windflower Letters-Correspondence with Alice Caroline Stuart Wortley and her Family")

Typical old-style headwear as seen on a picturesque bench in
Timisoara.

A faded beauty in Timisoara.

The Orthodox Cathedral in the centre of Timisoara, scene of the 1989 massacre, with the bent cross in front commemorating it.

Chapter 5

Elgar in Timisoara, Romania - October 2016

The air outside the airport was fresh and crisp but not cold. It was 11pm Romanian time but only 9pm in London. I made my way out of the terminal heading for the line of taxis waiting outside. I knew now would be the time to bargain and find the best deal as this late at night all the taxis were looking for a good fare. After much negotiation, I managed to lower the fee to something acceptable. It was still extremely cheap. Back in London, it would have bought me only a coffee and a sandwich.

As we rushed through the empty roads I started to observe the outskirts of the city. Everything looked different from Bacau. The roads were good. There were quite a lot of factories and distribution centres, and unlike Bacau, these were fully operating.

As soon as we entered the city I noticed the lights. The city had lights, and the lights had something to shine upon, lovely buildings that reminded me a lot of central European cities, Prague, Bratislava, Vienna.

The taxi parked in front of Timisoara Hotel, a belle époque building but one that from the inside looked very much like any modern 4-star hotel in the civilised world. The lobby was well lit and the bar was full of business people having a drink.

This place felt alright. I was already comfortable and excited about what was to come.

It was 12.30am and I had to start the rehearsal at 10, which meant 8am my time, which meant I had to wake up at 6am to get ready for my day.

I went to bed watching the BBC Channel, my closest, most comforting friend wherever I go.

There was a lot of discussion about the US Presidential elections and the third public debate between Clinton & Trump, yet that world seemed so far away from where I sat. Why do I always feel I go back in time when I travel to central European cities? Is it the architecture, is it the people or just my mind playing tricks?

The morning came, not surprisingly, too soon. I was lost in a deep sleep when the alarm went off and automatically I pressed the remote control and switched on the television, the same BBC Channel. They were still completely wrapped up in the Trump/Clinton campaign. They were discussing one of the famous tapes, then showed a press conference where yet another beautiful woman was accusing Trump of inappropriate behaviour. It could have easily been a Jerry Springer or Jeremy Kyle show with those dreadful wannabe actors having a go at each other, utterly trash TV. It is quite amazing how the human race can be degraded to such levels. It reminded me of a book I read in the summer which made quite an impression for the simple reason that it rang so true. Ben Elton's Blind Faith created exactly the same reality, or rather, virtual reality, where people spent their time sharing trash, and as a result, the whole human race was completely immersed in it. The next news on TV was about the attack on Kim Kardashian, the reality superstar. I have no idea why she is one. The thieves attacked her in her room and stole millions of dollars worth of jewellery, they had used her social media to locate her. It seems quite ironic that the thing that made her famous, was also the reason for her misfortune. Or is it? Maybe it is a blessing in disguise, now she has material for another reality TV show, talking about her misfortunes and the underworld of crime.

Only towards the end of the news was there a short piece about Syria and the Russians preparing another attack on Aleppo.

I was finally awake and in a state of puzzlement, partly due to the early morning, and partly to the news on TV. I got dressed and headed for the rehearsal hall.

Outside the sun was shining. It was a beautiful day. As I left the hotel and headed for the centre I had a good look around and tried to take in the atmosphere. This was a lovely city. Most of the buildings in the square dated from the 18th century and some were Belle Epoque. They were in great need of some investment and renovation but that aspect only added to my delight. I don't like shiny and perfect cities. They remind me of Romanian philosopher, Mircea Eliade's little essay about "Perfection". He describes the *Perfect Act* as a *Dead Act*. He considered perfection, not a path worth taking as it leads to an act that can be easily forgotten. We remember best things that are not perfect, actions that are flawed because our selective minds leave out things that are too uniform and orderly and remember exceptions. Age gives cities a dramatic effect, which is why places like Venice and Florence seem even more beautiful because of their imperfections. Timisoara embodies the same qualities. The top of the buildings were adorned with beautiful sculptures and ornate balconies, the colours were faded and in many places, they looked almost unsafe, but I loved the whole feeling of this place. I wouldn't change a thing, I would just make sure those sculptures and balconies didn't eventually fall. This state of decay was full of drama. Time had only made things more attractive. At the end of the main boulevard, there was the most beautiful Orthodox church, one of the prettiest I had ever seen, with beautiful red bricks and green, red and gold motifs on the towers. The towers were not identical but a combination of round and square. It was exquisite and I couldn't take my eyes off it.

The Philharmonic Hall was to the left of this church. It was not impressive and inside seemed similarly derelict, but on a closer look the building was interesting and the hall had charm. I went upstairs to the conductor's room which overlooked an open-air theatre and the park situated at the back of the hall.

Although I thought I was awake it didn't take me long to realise that the muscles in my hand and arm were not yet ready. Everything felt strenuous. I had to join the orchestra in 30 minutes and I felt so rough. I could hear the members of the orchestra already warming up, one horn player doing arpeggios, one violinist playing the beginning of Paganini 1st violin concerto. This felt good, always a good sign when the orchestra members come early and take the time to warm up.

These days I had a very different view regarding playing the violin. I wish somebody had explained that to me years ago. Playing a musical instrument is not a partial thing, it is not only the arms that are utilised. The entire body works towards a common goal of being able to perform at its best. It just happens that the arms and hands are the visible players, just as important is the spine, the shoulders, and even more, essential parts are the breathing and the mind. We know so little about this. In the hours that we spend practising not much is said about the way the body reacts and how integral the movement is. Teachers never incorporate gravity in the equation, and these days all I can think of is gravity, the way we use it, the way we bend it, the way we should respect it. I am sure great wizards of the violin, such as Paganini, must have had a very clear vision of how they used gravity to their advantage, like Usain Bolt, the athlete, they knew how important the laws of nature are to achieve a virtuosic performance. But here I refer not so much to the virtuosity as more to the wellbeing of musicians. They talk about stretching before performing and after, but nobody talks about the way different limbs or parts of the body, such as the hips, or knees can help you relax, and improve the way we can use gravity. I started observing this aspect and thinking constantly about it when I realised that shifting on the violin is not a movement of the arm but of the entire shoulder and the more relaxed the spine is the better the shifting will be. Or how the movement of the bow in the right arm creates all the tension on the left arm, which in turn makes a blockage in the tissue of the left shoulder, hence the many problems we violinists experience.

In any case, I just knew that 30 minutes were hardly enough to warm up the invisible parts of my anatomy and I just had to accept that.

I made my way to the hall. Everybody was in place and the conductor was arranging his score on his stand. I moved towards him, a little nervous, and said hello. He was a Frenchman in his 60s, distinguished looking with the most elegant specs, exactly my style, vintage and a little eccentric, totally signalling a particular need for beautiful and special things. He had good taste. He greeted me nicely but was not overly friendly. There was a distance he was very keen to keep.

He was conducting the Elgar Violin Concerto for the first time. This was going to be interesting. The orchestra started the famous long introduction that brings the most important musical ideas and highlights the virtuosity of Elgar's orchestrating. There are few composers who offer more brilliant and virtuosic writing for the brass section than Elgar. Suddenly, from being a supporting act, the brass section, especially the lower ones become the stars of the show. You immediately notice how the entire section, that usually dormant section, dominated by bored musicians who like to drink a little more than usual, mainly because they have so much waiting to do, were all invigorated, excited, scared, thrilled, stressed and alive. One composer had shone a light on them. The tempo was quite fast. There was a tendency of powering through it all without taking in all the little gestures that Elgar so diligently writes on the score. This started to worry me. The orchestral introduction came to an end and I prepared my entrance with my very own recitativo-like introduction bringing in the first Windflower theme. I didn't have much time to emphasise any of the pauses or *ritenutos* in the score as everything moved a little quicker than my own pace. I decided to follow. It was hard. We were moving towards something that didn't sound like Elgar anymore, it was driven, it was muscular, it was powerful but without the elegance and delicacy of his sympathetic writing. It felt too 21st century to me, and I liked period style. Still, I decided to follow the lead of the conductor. It was a tiring run through but the piece felt much shorter and concise. I was wondering about these feelings when we finished. The conductor seemed satisfied. He thought it was all going well and without major difficulties, except for the cadenza which from his reaction I gathered didn't make much sense to him, not yet. I felt exhausted and a little frustrated. I pointed out a few places where there were tempo changes which the orchestra had missed that I thought would make things a little more organic. Still, I had to admit, there was something attractive in this experience. Despite the lack of details in the approach, I could sense another perspective that could lead to something. There was no doubt the orchestra was good and there was a lot of potential there. The conductor liked things to have a flow and I didn't completely disagree with him. There is a very fine balance between avoiding the details and getting lost in them. An instinct told me to open myself to this new experience and embrace it rather than reject it. We didn't talk much about the game plan with the conductor. It was obvious he wanted to follow a clear path that he thought was right. I did feel a little left out of the equation but on some levels, I felt relieved. Everybody thinks this is a concerto for the violin but in reality, the real star in the piece is the conductor who has the task of creating a strong and organic bond between the orchestra and the soloist. This work is a mountain with many peaks, it is a symphony with a soloist, it is not a concerto. I decided to go with the flow.

The orchestra took a break of 20 minutes and I was approached by the first percussionist to join him and the conductor for a coffee. This was my first meeting with one of the members of the orchestra. He was a very jolly musician, full of spirit and self-importance. It seemed the conductor knew him quite well and they had mutual respect for each other. I genuinely thought he was the director of the orchestra. It is often common for members of the orchestra (usually brass or percussionists) to become directors of the orchestra. It is a good way of controlling things from within. It is also common that they rise to become music directors of philharmonic orchestras, a clear indicator of the time they have on their hands. The string players most of the time are too busy practising to fight for any other position.

I left the Philharmonic Hall with a great sense of relief that I was playing this concert now and not a year ago. I was ready for this challenge, I didn't think I could have coped with such demands earlier in my journey.

I made my way back to the hotel through the beautiful square. The sun was shining on the buildings and the cathedral looked stunning. I noticed a big stainless steel sculpture in front of it in the shape of a cross but quite a distorted, abstract one. I loved the emotional power of this bent cross. This had been the main square where the revolution of 1989 had started, the revolution that marked the end of the most brutal totalitarian system in Eastern Europe. My imagination was fired up and I was very keen to know more about the movement. It is quite sad to realise how quickly we forget the enormous effort and the sacrifice made by a few for the essential things most of us take for granted today.

I couldn't indulge for too long in the history of Timisoara. I was exhausted, in great need of sleep and practice.

I spent the rest of the day in my room, and in the intervals between sleeping, practising.

The next morning I was much better prepared for the day. After a long sleep things seemed quite different. I was ready to play by 10am. It was the general rehearsal. This time we started the rehearsal with the end of the third movement, the cadenza. In this concerto, Elgar does something very unusual. The common practice is to have the cadenza at the end of the first movement. It is a way for the performer to showcase his virtuosity on the instrument and produce variations on the different themes of the concerto. I often thought this process made the first movements much more important than the rest, the other movements were usually a beautiful song in the second and a joyful dance in the third. Elgar turns things on its head. He looks at the violin concerto as a much grander form, of operatic proportions. He brings the thematic motifs into all the movements and builds them and repeats them in different configurations, colouring them and giving them very different dramatic connotations. It all goes to show his incredibly creative and inventive mind. It is not easy to change the way you look at a form established for hundreds of year, giving it a fresh and unique expression.

He starts the third movement with a mysterious bubbly little passage transitioning into a very dramatic recitativo-like second theme and keeps developing the dance with interludes of beautiful chords in the wind section. Episodes from the first movement keep returning in this movement, sometimes the solo part stating them in chords replacing the orchestra which would have originally played them. The third movement is the longest and just as you feel he has exhausted all the permutations of the thematic material the orchestra transitions into the cadenza which picks up the same motifs from the first movement, this time in a different mood. The orchestra accompanies the violin with amazing sound effects using the instruments in an unconventional way and most of the ends of phrases are accompanied by chords in the winds. Again, in Elgar's eyes, this is a cadenza for the whole orchestra, not only the solo instrument. The conductor was very keen to perfect all the details in the cadenza and we worked on that for quite a while before having a general run through.

Already the orchestra was much more comfortable with the piece. They were focusing more on the dynamics, continuously encouraged by the conductor to really focus on every detail in the score. Although the tempos overall were slightly more fluent, I noticed that the fast passages were more in control and not as fast as on previous occasions. This gave me an opportunity to really focus more on the shape of these fast passages and create better climaxes at the end of big sections. In the second Windflower theme, most conductors slow down and disregard Elgar's notation *Semplice* and *A Tempo*, while in this case we just carried on as if this needed to flow. We left the music to speak for itself, simple, not cherished or elaborate, we just let it be. And I loved it, It was so much better, easier, logical, organic. We started the second movement in the right *Andante* tempo, again, a simple walking pace, playing less ourselves and more Elgar.

The third movement started in a more comfortable tempo, which I found almost too slow but in which the climaxes could unfold much better.

(Track 9 - Third Movement - First Theme)
https://aldadizdari.co.uk/elgartracks/track-9/

The greatest benefit was that my mind couldn't settle for just anything but had to constantly work on a new way, be open to taking a new point of view and as a result give a much more invigorating account of the piece. This was good, this was indeed something I was looking forward to.

I couldn't wait for the performance. I felt the pressure even higher because of these new horizons. I wanted to do well, I wanted to play my best. I wanted to combine all the details I had so diligently worked on for years and move them in this new direction, with more flow, more energy and let the music speak for itself.

During the break, many musicians came to congratulate me and wish me luck for the evening. They were genuinely pleased with my performance. They liked me, I could feel it in their smiles. It was a great feeling. Musicians are not the easiest people to please. They have expectations, they get frustrated, they need justification for the reason you are there in front of them, performing as a soloist, why is it you and not them? You have to earn your place, and that is fair enough.

(Track 10 - Third Movement - Second Theme)
https://aldadizdari.co.uk/elgartracks/track-10/

I went back to the hotel thinking about the rest of the logistics, sleeping, eating and getting my dress ready for the evening. I had selected a beautiful yellow dress for the evening. It was a dress I loved because of all the fond memories it was connected to. I had performed Mendelssohn's Violin Concerto in Lublin, Poland in that dress. It was the first time I had been in a place with Minus 20 degrees outside. I could still remember the journey on the train from Warsaw to Lublin in February. The endless fields outside covered in snow reminded me of novels by Solzhenitsyn. I had worn the same yellow dress for my performance of Brahms Violin Concerto in London, and then again for the live recording of this concerto in Kent.

People think clothes are superficial, but there is nothing superficial about concert dresses. Yes, they are produced to enhance your ego, but in reality, they become part of the story, of your most precious moments. Over time you see them and they remind you of the strongest emotions a human being can experience. They bring back the music, the journey, the people who helped you realise your dreams. In my case, I preferred vintage dresses, they added another layer of human experience which made them even more special. Like the city I was visiting, they were imperfect, yet beautiful.

There is one more ritual that I believe most instrumentalists enact before a performance, one that has almost religious importance and that is the cleaning of the instrument. The ritual can take up to an hour with every millimetre of the violin being polished and the strings being rubbed until there is no residue of rosin left on them. Not only are their violins the most beautiful objects ever created by human beings, in a violinist's life they represent an almost godly presence. We pray for them, to them, we argue with them, we curse them, then love them again, adore them. They are eternal, we are not. We just live through them for a lifetime and then pass them on to another soul. They vibrate to our life's energy and the more we give them, the better they resonate. They are the kings, we are the servants. This is why the insurance on violins is relatively low, considering the value.

After completing all my pre-concert rituals I made my way to the hall with plenty of time to spare. I wanted to warm up properly and have time to focus on my breathing. I was nervous, excited, a little scared. But above all, I felt a huge responsibility of giving the best I could and reaching another level in my rendition of this work. I had some pictures of myself taken backstage, warming up. This was always done reluctantly. I have a particular dislike for social media. This intrusion into people's lives, to me represents the first step towards the violation of our freedom. And I am somebody who knows very well how fragile freedom can be. Everybody wants a little of everybody else's freedom. I felt that so strongly in communist Albania, I felt it in Romania too, and almost as strongly in the States, which was absurd, as the US was supposed to be the land of freedom. Social media gives people a cheap thrill for the ego and takes away a big chunk of their freedom. Still, I took a few snapshots, if only for my mother to have something to pride herself on to her friends on Facebook.

I made my way to the backstage area and met the conductor who greeted me in a perfectly respectful and distant manner. We wished each other good luck and made our way on stage. We had a very good size audience. I was pleased to notice every member of the orchestra seemed perfectly concentrated and the sound came out strong and direct. The music had a nice flow, still a little uneasy at times, in my opinion not Edwardian enough, but most things had settled nicely. We needed a few more performances with this piece and then we would have come closer to Elgar and his world. But isn't that the case always, we always want a second chance, to make things better, to improve them. And yet, as Eliade so beautifully said, isn't life much better imperfect, isn't Elgar's music a great goal to aspire to, like a vision, the closer you get to it the further away it seems? And isn't that the beauty of everything? We were all in tune with each other and we had a very strong leader, our conductor had the intellect and stamina to deliver this work. As we transitioned from section to section, we repeated the motifs giving them different gravitas and colour, until finally, we arrived at the cadenza, the trigger point. It seems ironic that the trigger point, the emotional climax, which is usually the loudest moment, in this piece is the tenderest one.

The pianissimo in this cadenza seems almost too emotional to touch.

Elgar considered this concerto to be one of his most emotional pieces and one of his favourites. The cadenza strikes straight into the heart, the place when, as a performer, you touch eternity. Every time I find myself there I feel I can't quite capture the magnitude of this beauty, it is just a vision. I did my best and we took the work through to the coda and finished the concerto with great panache. The reception was extremely enthusiastic. They called me several times back to the stage and I decided to play a little encore. I hadn't prepared anything, Elgar is almost too much to take and most times I refuse to play anything, as nothing quite fits after such a journey. But, I thought, if there was a place where I could play something and if there was anything to add, that something would be by Enescu, the Romanian genius. He had played a vital part in the premiere of this concerto in Paris with Yehudi Menuhin as a soloist, preparing the orchestra prior to an elderly Elgar appearing for the performance. He loved the piece and was deeply disappointed by the cold reception it received. It seems the audiences there couldn't understand this new vision for a form of personal exposure such as a concerto, turning it into a form of operatic proportions. But Enescu could, after all, he spent most of his life writing his only opera, Oedipe, a masterpiece which is unfortunately rarely performed around the world.

It was very nice to see the change in reaction to me of the conductor after the concert. He invited me for dinner and was quite transformed. Was it our fruitful collaboration that convinced him to give me a chance and allow me into his well-guarded universe? I didn't waste time analysing the situation but happily accepted his invitation. It turned out, he was quite nervous about the performance himself. After all, it was his first performance of this concerto. We did have our differences of opinion about the music. The conductor lived in Vienna and was convinced the concerto shared a lot of things with Bruckner, whereas I was more inclined to believe Wagner and Brahms were the two strong pillars. In retrospect, I believe we were both wrong. As Elgar's close friend Billy Reed said in his book *"Comparisons of this sort seem futile; one might as well compare oak-trees with elms, or beeches with chestnuts, as seek to appraise the worth of one great master by comparison with the work of another"**. Elgar creates a world of his own. That world didn't come out of nowhere but what is an absolute is that it belongs in the Malvern Hills and it is filled with a pure Britishness that foreigners talk a lot about but can't quite capture. They think it is the Queen and tea, but if you ask me, it is Elgar and the Windflower themes.

I woke up the following morning with a bittersweet taste. I had played the concert, and it was time to go. My only consolation was that my flight was late at night and I had all day to explore the surroundings. The conductor knew the place very well. It was his favourite city in Romania, and now it was mine too. He suggested lots of places I had to see. The city had been under the protectorate of Maria -Therese of Austria and it had the most varied community of inhabitants, from German Protestants to Roman Catholics, Serbians, Hungarians and Jews, and they all had their churches almost on the same square. The squares were grand and after reading the plaques on the buildings it was obvious that a lot of successful master builders, gilders, architects and stone masons of the Austro-Hungarian Empire treated themselves to a big house in this city which stood at the crossroad of the Empire. My eyes were still full of the Orthodox Cathedral though, and I went to a souvenir shop and tried to find an etching or a good photograph of the Cathedral to take back home. I was not lucky enough to find anything that came close to the beauty of this building and, disappointed, I expressed my frustration to the shop assistant. I also mentioned to her how beautiful it had been inside. I had felt more meditative there than in other western cathedrals. She listened to me attentively but said: "It is indeed a very beautiful church, but for us, it has another side, a dark one. During the days of the revolution in 1989, the place in front of the cathedral, the square you see outside, was where people gathered to declare their freedom in The Proclamation of Timisoara. The streets were full of crowds, men, women, children. The army came and surrounded the square and started shooting. People rushed to the cathedral but the doors were shut. The priests had locked them. The women and children stood in front of the men in an attempt to protect them, hoping the army would spare them. But they didn't, they killed them all, and then most of the bodies disappeared so that the news would not spread that a revolution had started."

This story sent chills down my spine. It explained the bent cross. Somehow I couldn't look at the building with the same eyes again, the romantic vision had been killed by sinister reality.

But I loved Timisoara even more. This city, these people, they had freedom in their hearts. A cruel system hadn't killed the flame. They used a sense of culture and civilisation to fight a monster, they could make the sacrifice, because they had freedom in their hearts.

I left Timisoara with the hope I would see it again. What a lovely feeling that is, to want to return to a place, to recreate the present in the future.

* in the preface of his book "Elgar as I knew him" by W.H.Reed

The Beautiful Alley with the medieval towers and old city walls.

Rehearsal in the Sibiu Philharmonic Hall.

The Humanitas Bookshop in the pedestrian area.

The eye windows of Sibiu looking out over the small square.

The author with Xavier Corbero in his sculpture garden in Barcelona.

Chapter 6

Elgar in Sibiu, Romania - March 2017

Another chapter with Elgar. The sixth performance, in the heart of what used to be the capital of Transylvania. Would number six be a tricky one? I thought silently while packing my bags. I was heading for the land of Dracula, this time only a few miles from the place of his birth.

I made sure to allow lots of extra time before departure to avoid any traffic disasters and made my way to Luton Airport, which by the time of my sixth departure from there had started to look more like a building site than an airport. There is a slight chance this place might improve in the future and who knows, by the 20th performance with Elgar this might not be the land of the ugly anymore, but a little international space for the beautiful people, with lots of lavishly decorated stores and restaurants inviting you to spend your hard-earned cash.

So far, no disasters. I left England in perfectly good order. I arrived in Sibiu half past midnight and the first surprise was the car from the Philharmonic Orchestra waiting for me at arrivals. It was such a welcoming feeling, an instant comforting thought of arriving in a place where somebody cared about me.

The drive through the silent night was similar to a thousand others, going into a foreign city, same suburbs, same alien feelings, and yet, some strange similarities that linked them all together. Was it the badly lit streets? Or the messy architecture? We finally arrived in the centre of the city, Hotel Continental Forum. A big, rather chocolate box hotel, with a pleasing appearance and well illuminated.

The second surprise awaited me inside the room. Although very spacious and larger than most hotel rooms, it had a very strange layout. Instead of a door to the bathroom, the whole place was an open plan with two glass cubicles, one for the loo and one for the shower, cubicles which allowed air to circulate in but unfortunately also smells to circulate out. The two cubicles were connected by a very luxurious screen made of glass. I couldn't believe my eyes. This was not a money saving exercise, this was clearly a design feature. Somebody had had the brilliant idea of offering a Psycho moment to guests, as they showered in the transparent cubicle devoid of any privacy. It was both funny and sad at the same time. I decided to put my mind at rest, switched on the TV, and went straight to my only friend in foreign lands, the BBC Channel.

The world had changed so much in the short time since I had lasted visited Romania. Back in Timisoara, Clinton and Trump were having ferocious debates followed by millions. Now we had a totally different story. Trump was President, his face, a devilish gift to the world, was a daily reminder that the world has changed forever. He is living up to our expectations, with all the controversies and confrontations.

The following day I didn't have rehearsals. I woke up to a bright and shiny day. I made my way to the breakfast room and was transported back in time with a food I had encountered, maybe for the first time, in Romania, Salami from Sibiu. I helped myself to a few slices of the famous dry pork salami, curious to see whether it would taste the same as the salami back in those days. The taste hadn't changed.

The third surprise in Sibiu came as a shock. I couldn't find my passport. As I returned from the breakfast room, I was looking for my wallet where I kept my passport, local money and my cards. It had disappeared. This was a first. I was trained very early on to travel very mindfully, never losing sight of my precious essentials, my violin, music, passport and money. I searched everywhere in the room, not quite believing such a thing could happen to me. I presumed the only thing to do was to speak to the authorities in the hotel. After long hours of waiting around and searching the cameras in the hall to no avail I called the Philharmonic office and asked whether I had left anything in the car that picked me up, the reply was negative. Everything was coming to a standstill, my thinking was completely preoccupied with the logistics of how to get to Bucharest to get new travelling documents. I had to make declarations to the police and cancel my credit cards. It was at this point I started to wonder if there was something devilish about number six especially here in Dracula land.

The Philharmonic office sent me the car to get to the police station and as I opened the back door, between the door and the back seat, there it was, my wallet with my documents and money. After around five agonising hours filled with suspicions and disbelief, I had recovered my documents and was convinced that the devil had definitely played a prank on me, he was somewhere laughing out loud. I felt quite guilty for silently accusing the hotel of stealing. After all, I had requested a search of the camera footage and asked uncomfortable questions that many would find offensive. Half of my free day was lost with negative thoughts and by the time I went out to enjoy a little fresh air, a feeling of guilt had completely overwhelmed me.

It was a gorgeous day, the first day of spring. Everybody was on the street, the market was filled with the small gifts that Romanians buy every year for women, small tokens to wish each other Happy Springtime. They call them *Martisori*. Most of the time they buy bunches of snowdrops or lovely spring flowers. Again, my mind travelled back to my first day of spring in Romania. On the 1st of March I heard about the celebrations and bought a few Martisori for my teachers. Without realising the gifts were only offered to women, I gave one to the male conductor who was thoughtful enough not to laugh at me and make me feel embarrassed pointing out that in Moldavia they gave Martisori to men too. How appropriate that my last performance with Elgar in Romania would be on the day they celebrated Springtime. The Windflower Themes had become by now indispensable to me.

Sibiu is probably the most beautiful city in Romania. It has stunning architecture and is situated in a part of the country filled with a rich history from the German settlers to the famous Dracula, Vlad Tepes (The Impaler), who was born not far from Sibiu. He ruled in Wallachia in the Middle Ages bringing wealth and prosperity to the region by being an unforgiving ruler and imposing harsh punishments on those stealing or creating problems for the trading routes which passed through there. Later on Sibiu became the capital of Transylvania in the Austrian-Hungarian Empire and the Brukenthal Palace, now a precious art museum with over 1,000 art treasures mainly from the Renaissance Flemish and Dutch artists, is a testament to the power this city once had. I learned quite a lot about this region when I studied the story of Vlad the Impaler as my very first history lesson in Romania. I was hooked on Romanian history as it was fascinating and complicated. Albanian history is mainly dominated by wars, and most of those happened during the 500 years of occupation by the Ottomans. Romania offered a much more interesting historical landscape with rich ancient history, Middle Ages civilisations and the most fascinating first and second world wars which saw Romania rich, powerful and subsequently ruined.

The city was founded by German settlers and named by

them Hermannstadt and it has been a centre of German minorities since medieval times. It is located in the most beautiful region of Transylvania, surrounded by the Fāgaraš Mountains of the Southern Carpathians on the horizon with a medieval fortress inside the old city where I walked through the pedestrian area and a market in full flow. On the main street I spotted a bookshop, "Humanitas". I had spent most of my time in that bookshop when I lived in Bucharest. The main bookshop in the capital was located in the old centre of the city, within a courtyard that included the bookshop, a record store, jazz club and an open-air beer garden. The courtyard was only 10 minutes away from where I lived and I visited it daily, sometimes just to browse through books, buy records, listen to the strange music they played or to collect some information from the newly found world of internet. In Humanitas Book Shop I discovered a world much larger than the one I left behind. There I didn't feel lonely anymore, I felt excited, invigorated, I felt special. My journey had a meaning, my life was going to be richer despite the loneliness.

Entering "Humanitas" shop in Sibiu again today, the same calm prevailed. Here and there you could see people seated in comfortable chairs, drinking coffees lost in their books. There were no laptops or mobile phones, or big earphones, only people with books.

Still overwhelmed by my guilt from the morning, I started to feel nostalgic for my love for books. I revisited the Romanian Literature section and was almost in tears when I saw the collection of poems by Eminescu, the poet who made me cry with his poem (Lucifer). It was the first poem I could understand in Romanian. One day one of my friends at school came to my bench and started reciting something in Romanian. I couldn't understand all the words and she had to translate each word and put them together for me until I understood the meaning. The poem was by Nichita Stanescu one of the modernist movement poets and from that day onwards he became one of my favourite poets and she became my best friend. We shared many interests, above all music and books. As I looked through the display on the shelves I couldn't help thinking about her, grateful for her generosity of spirit and for making me part of her culture. Through music and books I found my true love for this country, my true gratitude to the Romanian culture, to their heritage. They gave me so much, they enriched and nourished me with something I couldn't find back home.

By the time I reached the big square my heart was filled with love for these people, for this country that I was rediscovering on a different level. I had discovered their heart through the books, now I was walking the squares of this beautiful land and was loving every stone on the streets. The big square had gorgeous buildings, really well preserved. Sibiu had been the European City of Culture in 2007 and the funding they received during that year had given the city a great makeover. Unlike other cities, such as Timisoara or Oradea, Sibiu didn't suffer from the dilapidated state of the buildings and everything, at least in the centre, was clean and colourful. The big square led into a smaller square, that in some way was far more intimate and elegant. The most distinctive characteristic in this city are the eyes on the buildings. The roofs of every old building have eyes, some two, others three and even five. They are so special, almost smiling, creating a feeling that at night the houses come alive.

The big square must have been the place where the rich lived and the smaller square where the merchants and craftsmen lived. The atmosphere of the city was one of calm, joy, and filled with young people. From the little square I could see the roof of a big church, the German Evangelical church and not far from there I could see the dome of a mighty

Orthodox Cathedral. I went to visit both and while the Late Baroque church was rather cold and austere, the Orthodox Cathedral was colourful, warm and very calming. From my experience of travelling around I realised that most of the interesting and magical places had been those that welcomed people from all kinds of backgrounds, where the society was a conglomerate of nationalities and religions, where the guiding rule was the law and respect for each other irrespective of religious beliefs and other cultural differences. The major empires, those that enjoyed great wealth and prosperity as well as cultural enlightenment, were always those welcoming cultural diversity, those that created a balance of forces and a backdrop on which people could build their lives. I feel the world we are entering now is starting to be much more divisive, less tolerant, less accepting and as a result, can only be regressive and oppressive. I had seen that only too well, during the communist years, those years when we just spied on each other and anybody who was different was ostracised.

The day ended with a very nostalgic meal of Romanian food, "Tripe Soup and Stuffed Sour Cabbage with Polenta and Sour Cream". It was a perfect day in Transylvania with a bit of devil's laughter and a big dose of Romanian love.

...

The following morning I had my first rehearsal with the orchestra. And the surprises kept on coming. As I faced the orchestra I started having a feeling of déja vú as I recognised some of the faces. It was a very strange feeling, as if I had been here before and had played with these people already. I had definitely met the co-leader, I was sure of that. He was a very serious individual, quite tall and not very friendly. I thought for a minute that my mind was playing tricks. It often happens that people remind me of other people. If you travel a lot, the mind starts making connections and I often played a game with myself, matching new faces with people I already knew. But, this was different, this was a little too much.

The conductor was an elderly Romanian from Iasi. He was quick to remark that he thought the orchestra had played this piece before, and there was not much point rehearsing it too long, therefore it all had to be done in one rehearsal, the general rehearsal. This already sounded alarming to me.

It had been a few months without that famous Elgar introduction and like a drug addict I was panting in anticipation, feeling almost like a charmed member of the audience rather than the performer, waiting impatiently to hear my favourite tune. And off we went. The music started, not perfect, not elaborate, but every bit Elgar. The landscape rises up, even in the toughest of terrains. The orchestra was not bad, they could certainly play. It was the conductor I worried about. He seemed unimpressed by Elgar's music, and that was a very dark idea to accept. He just rushed through everything, sweating like mad and waving his hands in all directions while the music became more and more impersonal, a long journey to the end with many missed opportunities and overall cluelessness. We didn't stop to work on anything, just played through so that he could see if he could get everybody to play together. We somehow did that, nothing more, nothing less. I found myself thinking about my first ever performance with this piece, in Oxford, with the amateur orchestra, and I missed them. I reflected nostalgically on the buzz and love those people gave, how they gathered everything they held dear and tried their best with the complex passages Elgar had written, every minute being conscious that before them stood a giant. I missed those feelings so much.

I do not believe music has a national identity that can only be understood by the people who share that identity. The truth of music transcends any barriers, language, cultural background, religious beliefs. I never felt that because Beethoven and Brahms were German, Elgar English, Debussy French and Enescu Romanian, I had no access to them. They spoke to me in the most powerful and sincere way, I embodied their national identity, for as long as I worked hard to discover the truth in their musical language and transformed myself and my sound to go beyond the possibilities of an instrument, searching for the poetry of the language.

I felt very sad playing in front of a good orchestra, surrounded by good musicians, who appreciated my efforts, but sharing the platform with a conductor who had not even bothered to properly study the score. The only remark he made about Elgar's Violin Concerto was that it was so thickly orchestrated and that cadenza so awfully written that he only hoped he would keep everybody together, as if that was a super mission, one given only to selected few. I had to sit there and listen unfortunately, as I do speak Romanian, to comments about Elgar's lack of consideration towards orchestration.

I didn't have the courage to tell the conductor that this piece deserved a little more love, more rehearsals, more than just an opportunity for the orchestra to flex their muscles while I rose up and down the fingerboard playing difficult passages. My distaste for flashy wizardry on the violin is clearer than ever. Like the books that I love, the world I long to embrace is the world of thoughts, images, colours and space. I long for my sound to be a palpable impression, bending and taking the shape of the ideas, the wizardry is not my goal. Ideas and feelings are the motivation for me, the only reason I am a musician.

The rehearsal finished before I could settle in and feel any strain. I was out of there in less than one hour.

During the break some musicians from the orchestra came and greeted me with much familiarity. They said they had played with me before, some in Ramnicu Valcea where a few months earlier I had performed The Lark Ascending by Vaughn Williams. Finally the mystery of the déja vú was explained. Most musicians in provincial orchestras can't make ends meet working in one orchestra, sometimes they play in several orchestras and hold simultaneously several positions up and down the country. This is the reality of classical music in Romania, it is a difficult world everywhere but here things are even harder and they work all the time just to be able to send their kids to school and cover their living costs. They said they really loved the work and had played the cello concerto before, but didn't know the violin concerto. I was fuming with anger and concluded the conductor was the worst I had ever worked with. His lack of curiosity and laziness made me almost sick.

I didn't have much time to dwell on my disappointment about the rehearsal. Outside the city offered a different perspective, much more uplifting and cheerful than the music. I came out into the most beautiful medieval alleyway. The concert hall was built over the foundations of one of the towers of the medieval wall around the city, most of which was still very well preserved. The towers and the walls stood high above the street named

"The Beautiful Alley", a reminder that this part of the world could once have compared with Carcassonne in economic and strategic power. It was truly glorious. The sun was magical, warm and welcoming. I walked back to the little square and crossed a beautiful old bridge that took me to some ancient alleyways where I found an antique shop. It was another sign that this city valued age. There were a lot of old artefacts, most of them German or Austrian and the shop was run by a very friendly lady. In two days I had met only pleasant people. I asked every person I met about their life in this city and they all replied they had been born, raised, studied and lived in the city all their lives and they were never going to leave it. They were contented with their lives. They were not rich, but they got by. I envied them, for their settled emotions, for their love of their city and their heritage. Back in Albania we couldn't wait to leave our country, we couldn't wait to reject our values and memories. What did it say about us? Did it mean I loved Albania less? The lady in the shop explained to me the story behind the old bridge that was named "The Liars' Bridge". According to the legend, the bridge was named as a result of the people getting into the market on Sundays. At the entrance to the little square they had to pay duty for their products and therefore most of them lied about the content they had in order to pay less tax. It sounded starkly modern.

Back in the hotel I was determined not to let apathy settle on the Elgar and focused on what I had to do. I had to communicate directly with the orchestra and inspire them to play their best and give this piece a chance. This was not just a very long concerto, this was as personal to them as it was to me. The conductor reminded me of a head of state. A very wise old man made a point to me once in a discussion about leaders and politicians in general, about their potential to change things. When I said that all politicians achieve nothing he turned to me alarmed and said: 'Oh no, Alda, you are mistaken, the point is not whether they do much good, the point is that they can do much damage'. Which is precisely what this conductor was doing to the music.

...

Concert day. I was not looking forward to the rehearsal, another run through, especially as I realised even more clearly how little the score had been prepared. I had to make a few remarks in order to make it easier for all of us to start various crucial sections together, particularly in the third movement, which is fractured and complicated. I succeeded in making my point only when the orchestra was all over the place and the conductor was sweating like mad but getting no results. His hands waving around like a badly coordinated bird unable to fly, despite all its efforts. In so many ways, this bad interpretation was giving me even more insightful information about the score that Elgar had written. As things were turning from bad to worse I couldn't stop thinking how easy it would all have been had we focused more on what Elgar had written in the score. It only took a close look to realise every sign, every comma, every rallentando or accelerando makes the score, that thickly orchestrated score, a friendlier place, makes the music flow in an organic way, gives musicians a chance to connect and gives them also a point of start and finish. All it took to give a reasonably good performance was a straightforward reading of the score, leaving personal takes aside. There is so much poetry in the little details in the score, so much emotion and pathos, you only have to look deeper. I thought to myself, if Elgar was here, listening to this rendition of his most beloved piece he would most likely have said: 'This conductor has gone off the boil'. This favourite expression of Elgar's put a smile on my face. I still hoped he would have found some humour in all this.

Finally, in the midst of the chaos, I managed to point out in the third movement that the comma just before the recitativo-like entrance by the solo violin was a chance for the orchestra to be together in the chord that preceeded that entrance. That detail noted, we were able to enter the second subject of the third movement in a more dignified way, together.

So, that was a useful rehearsal, after all.

The short rehearsal gave me another chance to wander around the city and head for the little square, by now a confirmed favourite place for me. I picked a bar/restaurant with some outdoor space looking out over the square and the view of the beautiful rooftops with the smiley eyes staring from above. As I was contemplating the beauty of this moment a Whatsapp message spoilt everything transforming my happy thoughts very quickly into sadness. My dearest friend, the giant artist Xavier Corbero, had had a heart attack and was fighting for his life. Now that view was going to be suspended forever in my memory, as the moment I found out Xavier was no more. No more trips to Barcelona, to his magical place, no more entering his land of freedom where creativity overtook every other pleasure. I felt as if those smiley eyes looking down on me suddenly turned sad and they reminded me of the strange windows Xavier used to install in his fantastic dream place. They were sometimes like eyes or mouths, opened into the wall, creating a weird and comical space where strange things could happen.

I had met Xavier eight years before and since my first visit he had become my idol. A close friend of Dali and the surrealist movement, carrying the torch of their creative expression well into the 21st century, Xavier had devoted some forty years to creating a magical space, a living sculpture that consumed all his creative spirit. The buildings were in themselves sculptures and sculptures were in themselves perfectly formed surreal characters. I adored him and all he represented. I had met my first genius, how many people can claim that in a lifetime? Around him I felt a free human being, even the violin felt it. When I played in his spaces the sound was different, as if transfixed or possessed by beauty. Although financial strains had characterised his entire life, given his taste for expensive and exquisite objects had no boundaries, one felt money didn't exist and was not an obstacle in his world, the only currency being freedom and the pursuit of beauty. And he knew it, he knew the effect he had on people and used them, abused them, adored them and drew them into his world with invisible chains made from surrealist dreams. He was like a magic bird that once you heard his song you were forever charmed. On several occasions, I went with him to the best restaurants, where, when he was on good form, I heard stories about the most famous people like Dali, Miro, Picasso and all their celebrated circle. The conversation would flow like a joyous liquor that got me completely drunk on life. After those lunches I felt I had been given some crazy energy pill that enhanced reality into some form of art. I recalled that once I almost said aloud that if death were to take me then, I wouldn't mind. I had lived such an incredible life and what was happening to me then was so profoundly beautiful. I had touched that fine line of life elevated into art that is almost unattainable, the artists' fine thread that one only has glimpses of. I had been part of it. And death didn't seem such a big deal.

That was Xavier for me, the man that defined life and death, and now he was facing it himself and I was far away, not able to do anything, just waiting to hear the worst.

I was seriously worried about the performance. My nerves were tense and I felt so hollow. It felt like the end of an era and waves of sadness swept over me. I went to the Orthodox Cathedral and sat inside, fully aware Xavier would not have approved of that, because he hated pompous religious demonstrations. In our conversations about faith he had often claimed he believed in God, because God was so wicked, he played the biggest pranks on us, and everything was absurd anyway. I could sense his relationship with religion was a twisted and complex one. When I visited him I often stayed in a dark green room filled with icons and little baby Jesus dolls looking down on me. It seemed like a nightmare you have as a child. The room gave me some very vivid dreams. I am sure Xavier knew there was something disturbing about this room, he liked to give his guests moments they would never forget, even if those included some nightmares.

Xavier Corbero, this little square in Sibiu and Elgar were tangled forever in the image of the end of a journey. Things that connected us all were all there. This afternoon was suddenly completely stolen by Xavier and it left almost no room for Elgar. I felt exhausted by my wave of emotions.

How is one to recover from loss? There are no words, no actions, no remedies. There is only time, that contracts and expands and for the longest time is connected only to loss and emptiness.

And then, there is music.

I went back to my room and was amazed at my ability to shut everything out and take care of the logistics of the evening ahead. You can always rely on autopilot playing. I liked this part of the exercise less and less, the more I believed in crumbling my walls with the audience the more I hated this autopilot feeling. I wanted my performances to be a pure connection and communication with no safety net. I had become much more adventurous. I didn't care anymore about hiding behind my ego and protecting things I once thought very important, such as pride. All that had somehow lost its appeal. What was the point of pride and ego when mortality is so close, and we have so little time anyway?

I didn't care about hiding my feelings these days, I felt I quite liked being raw, even if that shocked the receiver, and I felt it did quite often, especially the young people. I adored youth and loathed it in equal measure.

All afternoon was spent resting, eating and preparing my

dress and hair and arranging meticulously my makeup. The last thing was the ceremony of violin cleaning which was executed with particular detail and zeal. By the time I had to leave the hotel I had completed every task needed for the evening, and yet Elgar was nowhere to be seen. The music had disappeared somewhere and what once was an unbelievable moment of tension and almost pain, felt now like a regular day job. I felt very disappointed with myself. Even sadness had disappeared, leaving only a complete blankness. I was numb.

As I walked on stage, to a full concert hall I made one last effort to wake up from the blankness and play this music that I loved so much. Nothing else mattered, there was only music. Death will take us all, one day. Great art can keep us alive and can give that glimpse of eternity. As the orchestra rose to the first climax, I woke up, with a strong sense of beauty and love wrapping me up. I knew this piece so well, all those performances, all those people, all those hours of rehearsing. The only thing that mattered was Elgar and his work. I let myself go completely free and played the most beautiful Windflower theme to date. It was as if the spirit of Elgar, Xavier, and everybody I had loved and lost entered me and the music became an act of joy, of celebration, a state of trance where humanity is filtered and resurrected. As if by magic I felt the orchestra reacting to me, we were communicating like extended bodies, despite the badly coordinated bird, our conductor, still failing to take flight. He was not important anymore. We had established another understanding and were listening to each other and reacting to each other's moves. I felt the musicians even more concentrated since they could not rely on the person conducting them. They did a marvellous job, especially the brass section. They gave that incredible support to the work and I am sure that by the time we reached the cadenza at the end of the concerto, they agreed with me. This

was the moment of magic, this was the song of all songs. And we all sang it, in perfect harmony.
(Track 11 - Third Movement - Cadenza)
https://aldadizdari.co.uk/elgartracks/track-11/

The concert was a huge success and I was called on stage many times. I knew we had done this together. We had shared a very special moment. Elgar had brought a deeper meaning into their lives, I was sure of that. And I felt proud because I had done my job.

On my way to the airport the next morning I couldn't help wondering how it would have been if we had had a better conductor who could give the right insight and guided everybody a little better. But then, in some strange way, I felt because of him, that experience had been stronger than anything else. It was as if we had shared a secret, without a translator, we had penetrated the meaning of music ourselves, without a guide, without help. There was something refreshing in that. We had stopped playing music and we had become it. I wouldn't have had it any other way. I was ready to leave this place in peace. (Track 12 - Third Movement - Coda)
https://aldadizdari.co.uk/elgartracks/track-12/

Acknowledgements

Big thank you to Jane Hannath without whom this book would not have happened. Thank you for designing the cover, editing and for all your ideas, suggestions and for believing in my writing even when I didn't.

Thank you to Ioana Goia for bookings in Romania and helping me return to a country that I love.

Thank you to my parents for being an inspiration for this book. I am forever grateful for all your love and support.

Thank you to all the orchestras and collaborators who made the concerts possible.

Thank you to the Elgar Society for their support with the project.

Thank you to the Elgar Foundation for permission to use their picture of the great man.

#0176 - 240918 - C0 - 210/148/7 - PB - DID2310528